Bert John Vos

The Diction and Rhymetechnic of Hartman von Aue

Bert John Vos

The Diction and Rhymetechnic of Hartman von Aue

ISBN/EAN: 9783744644952

Printed in Europe, USA, Canada, Australia, Japan

Cover: Foto ©Thomas Meinert / pixelio.de

More available books at **www.hansebooks.com**

THE DICTION AND RIME-TECHNIC

OF

HARTMAN VON AUE

A DISSERTATION

PRESENTED TO THE BOARD OF UNIVERSITY STUDIES OF THE
JOHNS HOPKINS UNIVERSITY FOR THE DEGREE OF
DOCTOR OF PHILOSOPHY.

BY

B. J. VOS.

LEMCKE & BUECHNER
New York and London.

H. Grevel & Co., London.
1900

In the following study it is proposed to investigate Hartman's diction and rime-technic, considered more especially as
tests of chronology. The Songs have been excluded: they
differ from the other works in department, extravance of rime,
metrical standard and length. They hence demand a separate
treatment, in which the autobiographical and personal elements
naturally play a far more important part than in the case of the
epics.

The basis of the work consists of two dictionaries, compiled
by the author, one a rime-index to Hartman, the other a complete dictionary for all the works except Iwein, the dictionary
of Benecke being used for the latter. Exhaustiveness, it is
thought, has thus been attained for all the categories treated.
It will be found that even where these are not new, it has been
possible in several instances to correct traditional errors.
While the study was made mainly from the point of view of
chronology, interesting phenomena have not been excluded
simply because they did not yield to chronological treatment:
marked divergence of usage has in every case been recorded.
The work, it is hoped, will thus possess a value independent of
its conclusions.

Too much importance has in the past been attached to
individual criteria: diction, as represented by a few selected
words, rime-breaking, masculine and feminine rimes, juxtapo-
sition of two accented syllables. One is naturally somewhat
sceptical towards results thus obtained: good method would at
least demand a line of argument to prove that the category so-

der consideration was trustworthy beyond all others. Hence there has been no general acceptance of any one of these views, and results that in themselves were of some value, have been forgotten because they were unduly emphasized. The supposition lying at the foundation of all these attempts, that every such rubric will show a sliding scale of percentages that will truly represent the poet's development and fix the exact date of production for each work, is certainly a mistaken one. Development is not so mechanical: it is organic, has life and is, therefore, influenced by other causes besides period of production, causes that may in the main be subordinate, but that nevertheless often counteract. All such evidence must hence necessarily be cumulative. In strict accordance with this principle the aim has first of all been to lay down the facts. If by some the material should still be deemed insufficient, a contribution at least will have been made to the ultimate solution of the problem. One of the sources of the present study, a rime-index to Hartman von Aue and Gottfried von Strassburg will soon be made accessible.

The following editions were used: Erec, Haupt, Zweite Ausgabe, Leipzig 1871; Iwein, Henrici, Halle 1891–93; Gregorius, Paul, Halle 1882; Der arme Heinrich, Paul, Zweite Auflage, Halle 1893; Erstes und Zweites Büchlein, Haupt–Martin, Zweite Auflage, Leipzig 1881. For Gregorius Paul's larger edition, and for Der arme Heinrich, Haupt's edition were also consulted, but it seemed better to use the later texts as a basis. To Bech's text, especially for Erec and the Büchlein, reference is frequently made.

Works referred to in the body of the essay by the name of the author only, are as follows:

Jaenicke, De dicendi usu Wolframi de Eschenbach, Dissertatio philologica Halensis 1860.

Mensing, Untersuchungen über die Syntax der Conces-

sivsätze im Ah- und Mittelhochdeutschen, Inaugural-Disser-
tation, Kiel 1891.

Monsterberg-Münckenau, Der Infnitiv in den Epen Hartmanns von Aue, Breslau 1863.

Naumann, Ueber die reihenfolge der werke Hartmanns
von Aue, ZfdA XXII, 35-74.

Paul, Ueber das gegenseitige verhältnis der handschriften
von Hartmanns Iwein, PBB I, 368-401.

Saran, Hartmann von Aue als Lyriker, Halle 1889.

Steinmeyer, Ueber einige Epitheta der mhd. Poesie, Er-
langen 1889.

DICTION.

By *diction* is here meant the occurrence or non-occurrence of certain words or word-forms in the different works. As such it may comprise usage or non-usage of a word in a certain function, but the discussion of function *per se* lies outside of its sphere.

Some of the work included under this head has already been done for Hartman. Part of it will be found in Jesuleke, and much lies scattered through the notes of Haupt to his second edition of Erec. Corrected where necessary these have been included in the present list. Naumann in his article ZfdA XXII, relies almost exclusively on Haupt. My own statistic for these words is not dependent on either Haupt or Naumann, the afore-mentioned dictionary forming the basis.

The arrangement follows the alphabetical order. Related groups have, however, been treated together, under the head of the word coming first alphabetically, compounds being given under the simplex. When needed, references indicate where each word may be found. In some instances the numbers of the lines where the word is found have been cited, in others, where this would have taken up too much space, or where for other reasons this did not seem necessary, only the total number of occurrences is given. The definite article is prefixed to nouns to prevent confusion with verbs or other parts of speech. Verbs are entered under the first person singular, as in Benecke's dictionary to Iwein. An asterisk prefixed to a number signifies "in rime." Thus, *die* *als* E. 15 times (*9*)" means that *die* is found in Erec in rime nine times and of a total of fifteen. The carrying out of this distinction was, in part at least, suggested by Steinmeyer's remarks. Epitheta pp.

5 and 15. The different works are cited in the order, Erec, Iwein, Gregorius, Armer Heinrich, Erstes Büchlein, Zweites Büchlein, the order in which just comparison may most easily be made. It was not found feasible to introduce everywhere, within the limits imposed, distinctions of meanings and usages of individual words.

Vocabulary is naturally influenced largely by subject; it is, however, often impossible to distinguish the thought from its expression; perhaps here and there words have been allowed to stand that belong to matter more than to form. If these subserve no other purpose, they may perhaps help to bring out and emphasize characteristic differences in subject-matter.

Again, existing differences may at times be solely or largely due to editing. While reconstruction of text lay beyond the scope of the present study, attention has been called to the matter wherever the above seemed to be the case, and in this way, some contribution may ndirectly have been made to textual criticism. Words occurring only once have been included wherever they seemed significant. They are rather numerous in Hartman, and it is dangerous to base on them any argument concerning spuriousness, as long as their frequency in admittedly genuine works is not examined. Words occurring several times in one piece and not found anywhere else have usually been noted, to enforce this point, although in many cases they possess no value from the point of view of chronology. Here and there a word has been given a place in the list merely to bring out a difference of usage inside and outside of rime in regard to the different works. In related groups words that in themselves show no divergence of usage, have frequently been admitted to bring out and enforce the difference existing in the case of a related word, serving to show at the same time that it is a matter of words and not of ideas. It is not to be understood that words treated under one head are perfect synonyms: often the one may be inclusive of the other, or they may be synonymous in only a part of their various meanings.

a f t e r (wege) E 6731, 9849.

diu a h t e E 15 *times* (*9); I 5 (*1); G 2 (*1); AH 2
(*1); 1 B 4 (*1; l. 607 *with Bech); 2 B 1.   Cf. mahte under
mac.

über a l E *12 *times;* I 6 (*4); G *4.

a l b e g a r w e.   See garwe.

a l s a m.   See sam.

a l s u s E *1513; I 25 (*none in rime); G 25 (*8; also:
Grêgôrjus, 7 *times*); AH 11 (*1).   Cf. sus.

diu â m i e E 6 *times* (*3).

der â m i s E 3 *times*.

a n d e r h a l p (adv.) E 1748, 7859.   Cf. jenhalp.

a n d e r s i t (adv.) E 8721.

a n d e r s w â E 16 *times* (*14); I 5 (*4); G *3.

diu a r b e i t E 25 *times* (*20); I 50 (*44); G 10 (*9);
AH 12 (*10); 1 B 5 (*2); 2 B *2.   der k u m b e r E 12
times; I 27; G 8; AH 1; 1 B 14; 2 B 10 (*1).   diu n ô t E
47 *times* (*33); I 73 (*53); G 30 (*21); AH 24 (*22); 1 B
16 (*8); 2 B *7.   diu s w a e r e E 12 *times* (*9); I 19 (*14);
G 13 (*17); AH *3; 1 B 7 (*5; l. 128 adj. with MS and
Bech); 2 B 11 (*7).

b a l d e (adv.) E *8 *times* (*1161, *3472, *5005, *5243,
*5710, *6858, *6983, *7244); I *5; G 3 (*2; *2317, *3340,
*2867).   d r â t e[1] E 22 *times* (*13); I 15 (*8); G 12 (*10).

---

[1] Bech with MSS A l b reads d r â t e; this would be
the only passage in Hartman where b a l d e occurs outside
of rime.

[2] See h â t e in the discussion of rime.   This accounts
for the few instances in rime in Iwein.

AH 1. *173; 1 B *901.　　g e d r â t c　AH *1238, *1346.
s c h i e r c　E 33 *times* (*9);　I 52 (*10);　G 14 (*1);　AH 7
(*1); 1 B 4; 2 B 2.　s n e l l e　E 2845, 4038 (*MS and Bech
differ*), 4717 (*MS and Bech* scine); 1 B *952.

b a l t[1] (*adj.*) E *5498, *8625, *9032; 1 B *631, *1827.
daz, diu b a n i e r E 7 *times* (*2).

b a r (*adj.*) E *9 *times* (fröuden, gnâden bar *2989, *6482,
*9595); I *3; G 1.

ich b e d a r f E *943; I 8 *times;* G 3; 1 B 1; 2 B 3.

ich b e d i u t c E 5 *times* (*4); G 1; AH 1.

ich b e g â n E 19 *times* (*14); I 3 (*2); G 14 (*10);
AH *1; 1 B *8; 2 B *4.

b e g a r w e.　*See* garwe.

ich b e g i n n e[2] E 127 *times* (*31), *with the infinitive*
117 *times* (*25); I 46 (*9), *with the infinitive* 43 *times* (*7);
G 36 (*8), *with the infinitive* 34 *times* (*7); A H 19 (*3), *all
with the inf.;* 1 B 12 (*8), *with the inf.* 8 *times* (*5)[3]; 2 B 4
(*2), *with the inf. twice (not in rime).*

ich b e h a g e[4] I 3 *times;* G 6 (*2); AH 1; 2 B *1.
ich g e v a l l e (—*please*) E 12 *times* (*5); I 4 (*3); G *2;
AH *1; 1 B 5 (*2).

ich b e j a g e E 16 *times* (*12); I 3 (*2); G 3 (*1).

mich b e l a n g e t E *443, *9619; 1 B *1880.

ich b e r â t e E *8; G 5 (*4; *as adj.* l. 3263); AH 3
(*2).

b e r e i t (e)[5] (*adj.*) E 27 *times* (*25; l. 1721 — *perfect,
complete;* 22 *times in the first half,* 5 *times in the second*);

---

[1] Jaenicke, pp. 8-9.

[2] Cf. Monsterberg-Münckenau, p. 115 f.

[3] 1 B 1877 is the only place in Hartman's text where
b e g a n outside of rime has manuscript-authority. Those
denying the genuineness of the 'Leich' do not seem to have
noticed this.　In rime E has 20 cases of b e g a n against 5 of
b e g u n d e, I 4 against 1, G 2 against 4, AH 2 against 0,
1 B 4 against 2, 2 B 0 against 2.

[4] Also Lieder *215,7.

[5] Also L *209,3; *215,8.

I 5 (*4); G *3; 1 B *6; 2 B *1.   g e r e i t (er) I 31 *Hans (*17; l. 7997 Henrici — bereit; in all cases except 7 several MSS give bo forms); G 5 (*4; MSS differ, as also Pauli, larger and smaller editions).   g e r e l t e (ade. I 143A, *360A; G *x328 (MSS differ), *3462.

b e s t (adj.) E 22 times (*21; 1 28 (*12); G 13 (*5), AH 6 (*3); 1 B 3; 2 B 9 (*1).

b e s u n d e r E 16 times (*12); 1 *3; G 6 (*2); AH *1; 2 B *1.

b i d e r b e (adj.) E 6 times (biderbe unde wis 2073; biderbe unde guot 2924, 3002, 3688, 4850; den vil biderben man 3720); I 18 (see Benecke); G 877 (einen biderben man), 1793 (sint.... biderbe unde guot); AH 4 (biderber man 747; 1423; die biderben 413; b. unde guot 1315); 1 B 1825 (b. unde guot); 2 B 369 (biderben man), 730 (biderbe ist). Not in rime. u n b i d e r b e E 6400; G 3720. Cf. vrum.

ich b i n; wir birn, E *4051.

ich b i n d e E 21 (*18; MS and Bech differ II. 6246, 4824; helm (huotelin) uf (abe) b. 6 times); 1 *5; G *2; AH 6 (*4; all of maget). ich e n b i n d e E *912, *1021, *9382; 1 B *1662. ich g e b i n d e E *263A (helm abe g.). ich v e r b i n d e E 6 (*5; *872, *940, *4252, *448A, *3143, 5248); G *130.

b l a n c[2] (adj.) E 2020, 7298, *7333, *7347; G *2916; 1 B *1725. Cf. wiz.

der b o r t e E 8 times (*2).

b o c s e (adj.) E 3 times (4885, 5924, 6094; MS also 8694); I 22 (*1); G 8 (25, 826, 3966); AH 3 (*412, 414, 415); 1 B 11 (243, 364, 564, 581, 747, 877, 1150, 1234, 1234, 1849, 1850); 2 B 619.

b r e i t (adj.) E 24 times (*18; hande, vingere, nagele, hares breit 1561, 7313, 7656, 7696, 7733, 8143, 6726, 8083); I 6 (*2; three times of walttore); G 5 (*1; eines vingers breit 1603); AH 4 (*3; eines hares breit 1101); 1 B 2 (*1).

ich b r i c h o. *See* zebriche.

ich b r i u t e E 4 *times*.

b r o e d e (*adj.*) AH 105, 696, 1139.

diu b r u s t E 14 *times* (*7; 11 *plural forms*); I 4 (*one plural form*); G 4 (*plural*); AH 1 (*plural*); 1 B 2 (*1; *plural forms*).

ich b u h u r d i e r e E *3083.

der b u h u r t E 1314, 2142.

der b u r g a e r e E *5 *times*; G 5 (*2).

c l â r[1] (*adj.*) I *2 *times;* G *3436.

ich c o n d w i e r e E 9869, 9994.

diu c o v e r t i u r e E *738, 2339, 10025.

diu c r ê a t i u r e I 2 *times* (*1); AH *1199.

ich d a g e[2] E *4 *times;* I *3; 1 B *1.   ich s w î g e E *5419 (?), 7493; I 8 (*2); G 2; 1 B 2.   ich g e d a g e E *5; I *1; G *1; AH *1; 1 B *1.   ich g e s w î g e E *2; I 1; 2 B 1.   ich v e r d a g e E *17 *times;* I *5; G *2; 1 B *4. ich v e r s w î g e E *3044; I 5 (*2); G 8 (*2); AH 1; 1 B 3 (*1).

der d a r m g ü r t e l E 818, 1453, 2028, 2798, 7681.

der d e g e n[3] E 11 *times* (*7); I 4 (*1).   der h e l t[3] E *1734; I 4 (*3); G *872.

d e g e n l i c h (*adj.*) E 8542.

d e i s w â r[4] E 2377; I 9 *times;* G (dêswâr) 11; AH

---

[1] Steinmeyer, Epitheta p. 7.

[2] d a g e n with its compounds confined to rime. g e - d a g e also L *214,s.

[3] Cf. Jaenicke, pp. 4 and 5.

[4] I take the editions as they stand. d a z i s t w â r (especially at the end of the line) and f ü r w â r often do not appreciably differ from d e i s w â r and z w â r e. MSS vary greatly. z e w â r e and z e w â r e are included in z w â r e.

(dôswâr) 1; 2 B l. 66 (MS xwar, Bech zwâro). zwâre E 14
(*1); I 51 (*5; Bennecke omits l. 441); G 8 (*4); AH 6; 1 B 6;
2 B 10.

ich denke E 14 times (*3; Bech, following the MS
writes 7 of these with ge-, leaving 7 (*3); 1 7 (see Bennecke;
Henrici has left 2 stand: 3861, 5977); G *1; AH *1; 1 B 1.
ich gedenke E 41 times (*16; Haupt's text: for Bech add
the 7 above); I 35 (*6; according to L²⁰; for Henrici add the
5 above); G 23 (*5); AH 10 (*2); 1 B 10; 2 B 2.

deste E 4 times (MS and Bech also 6373; MS 6433);
I 17 (Henrici 20 times); G 7; 1 B 2. di u with comparatives
E 6372 (MS and Bech deste), 6433 (MS deuter); I 3 times
(Henrici with MSS deste; 2369, 2653, 4395 A die).

dicke: ofte E 35 times (*6; MS and Bech also 6254;
: 3 (5032, 7067, 9156); I 23 (*3) : 2 (3049, 7528); G 9 (*1)
: 2; AH 1 : 1; 1 B 13 : 3; 2 B 0: 3.

dienesthaft (adj.) I 4 times; G 1091; 1 B 1073.

doch[1] (concessive conjunction) E 9 times; 1 B 709.

drâte. See balde.

draete[2] (adj.) 1 B *1858.

der drozze E 3295.

eben (adj.) E 5146, 7840, 8708. ebene (adv.) E
1899, 6719, 7319. ich ebene E 3216. ebenriche
(adj.) E *9106. der ebenwâc K 7796.

diu ecke[3] E 9960.

---

[1] Cf. Haupt on Erec 943, Naumann p. 34, and Menning
p. 34, who all omit E 591. Menning (to judge from the
numbering he is influenced by Bech's note on the passage) also
counts E 593, but doch is there adverbial. The other omis-
sions of Haupt are silently corrected by Menning l. c. Also
L 208,24; 216,16.

[2] Might have been added to Saran's list p. 66.

[3] Cf. Jaenicke p. 19.

e d e l (*adj.*) E 39 *times;* I 13; G 5; AH 1.

e i n e (*with preceding genitive - without*) E *2317; G 3104, 3137.

daz e l l e n[1] E 6 *times;* I 1; G 1; (2 B 497, Bech). e l l e n t h a f t[2] (*adj.*) E 660, 9606, 9676; G 2170. e l l e n d e (*adj.*) E 12 *times* (*6); I 2 (*1); G 9 (*6). daz e l l e n d e E *4 *times;* G *1; 1 B *1.

ich e n b a n 1 B (*1652 *MS and Bech.* Cf. Schönbach p. 383; 1665 *MS and Bech, Haupt* er-) *1749.

ich e n b a r G *571, *1650.

ich e n b i n d e. *See* binde.

e n b o r (*adv.*) I 4 *times* (*2).

der, daz e n d e E 35 *times* (*12; es an ein ende komen, etc., 1234, 3244, 6005, 6779, 9411); I 17 (*2); G 15 (*5; es an ein ende komen, *1371, 2368); A II 4 (*1; es an ein ende komen, 548); 1 B 3 (*1; es an ein ende komen, 92); 2 B 1.

e n g e g e n. *See* gegen.

e n m i t t e n (*adv.*) E 12 (*4; l. 9203 *MS and Bech different*); I 2; AH 1.

ich e n s c h u m p f i e r e E 2648, 2660, 2697.

ich e n t ê r e. *See* unêre.

ich e n t h a l t e (— beherberge) E *315, *9966.

ich e n t s t â n[3] E *1232, *6453, *8111; G *193, *405; 2 B *135, *676.

e n f r e i s e. *See* freise.

e n w â g e (*adv.*) E *5479; 2 B *158.

ich e r b e i z e E 13 *times;* I 3; G 1.

ich e r g â n E 43 *times* (*35); I 22 (*19; l. 7476 *with Henrici*); G 15 (*10); AH *7; 1 B *13; 2 B *3.

ich e r g e t z e E 8 *times* (*5); I 2; G 3 (*2); 1 B 1. Cf. ersetze.

---

[1] Jaenicke p. 20.
[2] Jaenicke p. 12.
[3] Also L *214,21.

ich u r h o b e E 3 *times* ("3; diu rede erhaben ist 4, 4411;
G S (diu unsere erhaben sint 673); AH 1; 1 B 1.

ich e r k i u s e E 14 *times* ("11); I "6; G "3; 1 B "2.

ich e r l e s c h e.   Nur kmebe.

ich e r l o u b e E 2890, "3207; G 1243.

ich e r l o u f e E 7173; G "1704; 1 B "763.

ich e r r ä t e (— treffe) E 9784, "4417, "9208.

ich e r r e c k e E 1464; G "802.

ich e r s c h e i n e E "6 *times*; AH "634.

ich e r s c h i n e E 7 *times* ("2); I "3931; 1 B 705.

ich e r s e t z e E "6349, "6393, "7373, "9777, "10070;
G "2179.

ich e r s i h e (entleere) E "5415, "5720.

daz e r t r i c h e E "5210, "5220, "9185; G "2013.

ich e r v ü e r e (swert) E 4398, 4704.

ich e r w i g e E "374, "849, "2673.

ich e r w i h e E "895, "5721.

ich e r z i u g e (— erzeuge, fertige an) E 1384, 2801,
7150, 7478, "8599, 8955.

ich g ä h e E 10 *times* ("7; 140, "1150, "2493, "2335,
3473, "3488, "4113, 6705, "6825, "9007); I 14 ("11); G 10
("5; "155, "953, 1381, "1853, "2151, 2519, 2084, 8079,
3084, "3323); AH "656; 1 B "1142, 1531. ich i l e [1] E 9
("1; 159, "3063, 3543, 4894, 4946, 5090, 5379, 6453, 10011);
G 2703. diu g ä h e E "3, "9376. diu g a e h e E 4109,
6676. diu g a e h e d e E 4190. diu i l e E "947.

g ä n z l i c h e n (adv.) E 6784, 7348, 9602; G "2471.

g a r w e [2] (adv.) E "6 *times* ("1700, "2835, "7392.

*7597, *7726, *8922). begarwe[1] E 5 *times* (*4; *325, 474, *1564, *1704, *5619); G *2 (*1949, *3851); 1 B *295. albegarwe E *1783.

der garzùn E 2518, 6715, 6816, 6825; I 9 *times.*

ich gearne E 1046, 1280, 4768[2]; 1 B 405.

ich gebâre E *2483; I 12 *times* (*9); G *228, 1553, 1762; A H *304, 1410; 1 B 802, 806.

diu gebaerde E 7 *times* (288, 6397, 6551 *with Bech*); I 10 (*2); G 2385; AH *991, 1286. gebâre[3] E *6 *times* (*1805, *3129, *5280, *5862, *6599, *9801).

diu gebe E *4557, *9535 (l. 7229 gibe *with Bech*); G *3890; A H 348.

ich gebriche. *See* zebriche.

ich gedenke. *See* denke.

ich gediene. *See* verdiene.

gedrâte. *See* balde.

gegen (*prep.*) E 31 *times;* I 5; G 7; A H 4; 1 B 3 (l. 100 *MS and Bech different*). engegen E 16 *times;* I 11 (*Henrici has restored* gegen, gein ll. 281, 5592, 5599, 6239); G 2.

gehaz[4] (*adj.*) I *10 *times.* vîent (*adj.*) E 5360, 5656; I 1.

ich gehille I 4 *times.*

gehinre[5] (*adj.*) I 1387.

gelich (*adj.*) (glich, geliche, gelich *etc.*) E 41 *times* (*18; ll. 9934–39 *contain* 12 *cases*); I 17 (*11); G 7 (*4); AH 4 (*2); 1 B 4 (*2); 2 B 3 (*1). geliche[6] *etc.* (*adv.*) E 34 *times* (*19); I 9 (*3); G 6 (*3); A H *2; 1 B 2 (*1);

---

[1] Naumann cites 4 instances. Including, as should be done, albegarwe, there are 6.

[2] Cf. I 4502.

[3] gebaerde not in rime in Erec; gebâre only in rime.

[4] Also L *207,₃₅. vîent L 209,₁₆.

[5] Cf. Steinmeyer, Epitheta, p. 12.

[6] See the statistic of rimes in îche.

2 B 1. algeliche E °1305, °2960. ungelich (adj.)
E 2 times (°1); I 4 (°2); G °2; 2 B °1. ungeliche (adv.)
E 3 times (°3); 2 B 2 (°1).

geliop (adj.) E 2208, 3018 (subst.), 5628 (subst.);
G 646 (subst.), 2550.

mir gelinget E 13 times (°10); I 5 (°2); G °2; 1 B
9 (°7); 2 B 3 (°1).

gelpf (adj.) E 1569 (rubin), 8108 (subst.), 4167 (Up);
I 625 (rubin); G 3391 (ongen), 3436 (ongen); 1 B 1718 (subst.

gemeit(o)[1] (adj.) E °9 times (°12, °2049, °3851,
°4596, °7214, °7669, °7609, °7732, °8075); AH °1172;
1 B °1657.

genaedeclich (adj.) E 8071, 8837; 1 B 1390, 1666.
genaedeliche(n) (adv.) E °1215, 2r88; G 8164.
genaeme (adj.) E 5 times (°4; °1775, °3740, °3671,
8346, °9895); G °2 (°632, °3422); AH °2 (°124, °3111.
ungenaeme (adj.) G 8551; AH °1477. Cf. genaeme.

ich genende 1 B °1690. genendic (adj.) E 2557,
7961; G 1951. genendeclichen (adv.) E °9718, °9045;
I 8760 with Henrici; 1 B 753; 2 B 914 (MS and Bech different). diu genendekeit E °2508.

ich genise E °13 times (the first instance °4244); I 32
(°27); G 22 (°15); AH 11 (°5); 1 B 4 (°2).

diu genist I 1288; AH °151, °260.

der genôz E °7 times (°117, °2109, °2418, °4284,
°8035, °9013, °10061); G °528; AH °1123; 2 B °233. ich
genôze E °9050; AH °464; 2 B °217. genôzsam
(adj.) E °3968; G °2597. diu genôzschaft I °1474.

daz geraete E °2; G °2.

gereit. See bereit.

geschaffen (part.) E °6630, 7353, 7833. geslaht
E °7583, °7746. gestalt E °7338, °7376, °8834; 1 5

---

1) Cf. Jaenicke p. 9 f., Steinmeyer, Epitheta pp. 14 and
20. Haupt on Erec 12 (quoted by Leitzmann, PBB XVI,
353) omits ll. 7669 and 7699. So Naumann p. 23.

times (*2) g e t â n E 18 *times* (*16); 1 5 (*3); G 7 (*5); AH *1: 1 B *2; 2 B *1.

von g e s c h i h t e n E 1864, 2652 (*Haupt* von geschihte, *MS and Bech* von geschihten), *5811 (von geschihte), 6133, 8716.

daz g o s i n d e E 1478, 2745; I 13 *times* (*5; l. *7858 *with Henrici*); G *1400. daz i n g e s i n d e E *308, *1274, 1282. 5696, *6051, *7770; I *twice* (*1); G 229; 1 B 621, *1052, *1812.

g e s l a h t. *See* geschaffen.

daz g e s l ä h t e[1] E *4523; G *1280, *1497.

g e s t a l t. *See* geschaffen.

ich g e s t â n E 9270; I 10 *times* (*5); G 8 (*3); AH 659; 1 B *1486. *1491; 2 B *134, *177, *652.

g e t â n. *See* geschaffen.

ich g e v a l l e. *See* behage.

ich g e v e l l e E *984, *5567. daz g e v e l l e E *5519.

g e v e l l i c (*adj.*) E 7540; G 2972.

diu g e f u o g e E 7541; G *1242.

daz g e w n e f e n E 3656, 4154, 4722; (*Henrici* I 5019, 5021).

daz g e w a n t E *9 *times* (*244, *297, *645, *1412, *1540, *3547, *3725, *4707, *5400); I *2 *times;* G ,10 (*8; *360 (= bettdecke), *975, 999, 1006, *1945, *1951, *2512, *2708, *2750, *3782). daz k l e i t E 6 *times* (*2; 1531, 1578, 1587, *2012, 3199, *9855); I 15 (*9); G 9 (*5; *103, *112, 285, 368, *1642, *1948, *2748, 3111, 3655); AH 3 (*2: *1022, *1191, 1193). diu w â t E 18 *times* (*11; *336, *359, *649, *1571, *1588, *1954, 1970, *1984, 2015, *2183, 3066, 5325, *8073, 8230, 9938, 9958, *9960, *10030); I *5 *times;* G 9 (*7; *711, *1094, *1161, *1559, 1743, *1812, *1942, *3384, 3482); AH *1194.

der g e w i n E 14 *times* (*12; *928, *1620, *1858, *2620, *2705, *3301, *3755, *4020, *7976, *8013, 8032,

---

[1] Only in rime with m ä h t e; see m a c.

8388, *889x, *9107); I *6 (4 *of three in section 253*; O 6
(*5; *1028, 1105, *1140, *1775, *2042, *3040); I B *1845,
*1592; 2 B *56, 108 (*varies*), *528.

g u z n e m e (adj.) E 1964, 9034. u n g e z n e m e (adj.)
E *3888, 4170. m i s s e z n e m e (adj.) E 3761. w i d e r-
z n e m e (adj.) G *3421, *3562; AH *123, *147s. CX. ge-
naomo.

ich g e z i m E 39 times (*331; I 6 (*4; *Ibn rird made
zimt l. 9691); G 5 (*6); AH 2 (*9); 1 B 5 (*3); 2 B *1.
ich z i m E 16 times (*6; MS and Bech ge ll. 364, *9141;
MS ge ll. *2745, 9626, 10035); I 9 (*3); G 3; 1 B 3 (MS
ge l. 1469); 2 B 2. ich m i s s e z i m E 4681, *6397, *7368,
*7451; I *4549; 1 B *59, *163; 2 B 427. ich t o me[1]
— gezim E 10 times (*9); I 9 (*7); G *3; AH *3; 2 B 2
(*1).

daz g o l t E 29 times (*11); I 9 (*4); G 13 (*7); AH *1.
g u l d i n (adj.) E 3 times (*2).

g r i m m e (adj.) E 10 times (*2; N3x, 884, 3291, *3297,
5568, 6663, *8993, 9139, 9153, 9284); I 2 (*1); G 1. *20.
diu g r i m m e (der grim) E 8 times (*5); I *4; G *3323;
AH 1285. g r i m m o (adv.) E 9680. g r i m m i e (adj.)
AH 1029. g r i m m e c l i c h (adj.) E 4 times (*1; 3004,
9082, 9211, *9352); I 1. g r i m m e c l i c h e n (adv.) E
6218.

g r ü e n e (adj.) E 9 times; G 1; AH 1.

___

ich h ä n; häte. *See discussion of rime in äre.*

___

[1] Of the three definitions given by Benecke, only the
first, b i n a n g e m e s s e n, is synonymous with z i m and
g e z i m. Although it is somewhat difficult to distinguish
sharply between these various meanings, the attempt has been
made above. Grouping them all together, as Benecke has
done, the figures would stand: E 14 times (*11); I 22 (*14);
G 8 (*6); AH *6; 2 B 2 (*1).

h a r t e[1] (*adverbial modifier of adjs. and advbs.*) E 4 *times*
(484, 1009, 3455 — harte vil, 4861); I 41 *times;* G 40; AH
15; 1 B 5; 2 B 3. v i l (*advb. modifier; comparitives excluded*) E 350 *times;* I 189 *times* (*1; *5589); G 102 *times;*
AH 62 *times;* 1 B 53 *times;* 2 B 9 *times.*

diu h e i d e E 11 *times* (*10); I *1; G *1; 2 B 2 (*1).

der h e l t. *See* degen.

daz h e r. *See* schar.

h ê r l î c h (*adj.*) E 5 *times* (*2; *288, 1212, 1937, 2067,
*3199). h ê r l î c h e (n) (*adv.*) E *1835, *2107; I 6448.

h e r z e n l î c h e (n)[2] (herze-; *adv.*) E 1261 (frô), 1303
(frô), 1846, 4018 (frô); G 2310, 3870 (frô). h e r z e n l î c h
(*adj.*) G 2491, 2705.

diu h e r z e r i u w e. E *4085, *4256; G 852, 2402;
AH 1028. h e r z e r i u w e c l î c h e (*adv.*) E 5745.

diu h e r z e s ê r e E *5 *times* (*5608, *5749, *6284,
*8677, *9692; AH *242.

h i n n e n (*adv.*) E 4697, 9464; I 13 *times* (*7); G 1713,
*3092; 1 B 1535; 2 B 613.

diu h i u f e l E 8318; G 2544.

ich h o e r e[3] E 20 *times;* I 31; G 13; AH 7; 1 B 7;

---

[1] In view of this marked difference of usage between Erec
and all the other epics, Haupt's emendations l. 2899 (MS and
Bech g a r f r i u n t l î c h e), l. 5500 (MS g a r s ê r e, Bech
v i l s ê r e) and l. 6442 (MS g a r s t a e t e, Bech v i l
s t a e t e), in all of which cases he reads h a r t e, seem very
doubtful. The principle expounded in his note to l. 5500,
does not suffice. It would first be necessary to show that there
had been a wholesale change of h a r t e to other strengthening
particles. Haupt himself has not assumed this. The same
applies to Bech's h a r t e s c h i e r e l. 3801 (MS r e c h t).

[2] See the statistic of rimes in î c h e. None of the above
are in rime.

[3] Excluding E *7551 (—aufhören) and the compound
h o e r e z u o. The latter occurs 8 times in Iwein; for the
other works the references are: G 3806; AH 198; 230; 1 B
1309; 2 B 183. E 8634 we find g e h o e r e z u o, which also
occurs 1 B 613 and 1215.

9. B 6. ich gehoere (—höre) E 6 times; I 9. ich vernim[1] E 67 times (°49); I 15 (°11); G 22 (°15); AH 4 (°2); 1 B 16 (°13.)

daz houbet E 36 times (°9); I K (°2); G 2.

hövesch (adj.) E 3517; I 15 times; AH 1. 74. die höroscheit E °3451; I 6 times (°3). hövesch-lichen (adv.) I 5894. hovelichen (adv.) K 2841. hovelich (adj.) 1 B 817.

daz hüetel E 8966 (Bech with MS huetiln). daz hüetelin E °952, °2640, 6953.

diu hulde E 6 times (°2; 132, °1251, 2587, 3459, °4077, 4976); I 25 (°20); G 12 (°7); AH 8 (°4); 1 B 2 (°1).

io (adv.) E 69 times (°9); I 75 (°7; 11. 2247, 2469, 4062 with Henrici); G 34 (°2); AH 12; 1 B 26 (°3); 2 B 7. iemer E 44 times; I 73; G 21; AH 11; 1 B 25; 2 B 14.

iedoch (adv.) E 6 times (1265, 3859, 3955, 6003 (MS and Bech doch), 7902, 9870); I 16 times (°3; including l. 2567); G 462, 1582; AH 5 times (347, 594, 600, 932, 1396); 1 B 5 (°1; 439, 984, 1453, 1564, °1622 (MS and Bech doch).

ieglich (adj.) E 19 times (4 adjectively, 15 substantively); I 3 (adjectively); G 4 (3 adjectively, 1 substantively); AH 1 (adjectively).

iemer. See ie.

ich ile. See ich gähe.

diu ile. See diu gähe.

der imbiz E °668, 2143, 9947, 6646.

daz ingesinde. See gesinde.

---

[1] The greater rime-facilities of vernemen partly explain its frequency in Erec, hoeren, with the exception of E °7551, not being found in rime. Still vernemen occurs 18 times in Erec outside of rime, while Iwein has only 15 inside and outside of rime.

daz i ꞅ e n (— rüstung) I 4 *times* (*3). daz i ꞅ o n g e- w a n t E *9 *times;* I *1. diu î ꞅ o n w â t E *4158.

der i t e w i z E 3 *times* (*2; *2258, 3001, *8273); G 3 (*1: 1369, 1491, *3634).

j â (*aꞅꞅev.* —fürwahr) E 33 *times;* I 14; G 28; AH 9; 1 B 22; 2 B 2.

j ꞁ e m ꞁ r l i c h (*adj.*) I 4 *times* (*1); G 2 (1327, 1820); A H 5 (*1; 261, 716, 991, 1032, *1286). j ꞁ o m ꞁ r l î c h ꞁ (n) (*adv.*) E 2 (*1; 5297, *8081); I 4 (*2); AH *130.

j e n ꞁ r (*pron.*) E 20 *times;* I 8; G 3; 1 B 2; 2 B 1. j e n h ꞁ l p E 5008, 7575. j e n e n t h ꞁ l p E 6864. Cf. anderhalp.

diu j u ꞁ t E 9 *times;* I 3 (tjost). ich j u ꞁ t i o r e E 11 *times* (*2); I 1 (tjostiere): G 2. ich g e j u ꞁ t i e r e E 2 *times;* G 1.

der k a m p f E 8632; I 24 *times;* 2 B 565.

ich k ê r e [1] E 23 *times* (*9); I 47 (*29); G 11 (*7); AH *3; 2 B 7 (*6).

daz k i n d e l i n [2] E *2868; G *472, *686, *708, 1051.

daz k l e i t. *See* daz gewant.

der k n a b e E 16 *times* (*1; — knappe 2344, 2507, 2639, 3058, 5123; — knabe 3491, 3499, 3510, 3541, 3559, 3575, 3590, 3596, 3599, 3644, *5553); I *5056 (— knabe). der k n a p p e E *2048 (—knappe); I 4 *times* (—knappe); G 3 *times* (— knabe 1273, 1286; —knappe 1723).

---

[1] The statistic for w e n d e (which is, however, hardly a synonym) is: E 25 times (*20); I 15 (*13); G 9 (*4); AH 6 (*2); 1 B 9 (*3; MS and Bech also *1681).

[2] See statistic of riimes in -i n.

der k n e h t[1] (= *knight*) E 81 *times* (*19; with the adjec-
tive gnot everywhere except 7080); 1 *5. der r i t t e r E 122
times; 1 83; G 14 (*1); AH 2; 2 B 2.

der k o l b e[2] E 5367, 5522, 5541; 1 2 *times*; 2 B 220.
k r e f t i c (*adj.*) E 4 *times*; 1 4; AH 1. k r e f t e e l i e b
(*adj.*) E 4 *times* (*2). k r e f t e e l l e h e n (*adv.*) K *512.

der k u m b e r. *See* diu arbeit.

k u m b e r l i c h (*adj.*) E 6 *times* (*1); 1 2 (*1); 1 B 2
(*1). Cf. kumber.

ich k ü n d e E 519, 5604 (ver. *Bech with MS*); G *690,
1018, *1749, 3755, 3910.

daz k ü n n e[3] E *1746, *9468, *9547; G *3147; AH *90,
*388, *656, 1170. daz m a n k ü n n e 1 B *720.

k u r z (*adj.*) E 15 *times* (*with frist, stunde, wile 6 times*;
1 26 (l. 1168 *with Bech and Henrici; with frist, stunde, zh,
wile, zil 20 times*); G 6; AH 1 (stunt); 1 B 1 (frist); 2 B 4
(*with zit 2 times*). kurze (*adv.*) E 2135, 6901, 6378, 4510.

daz l a s t e r[4] E 11 *times* (*1); 1 23; G 2; AH 1; 1 B 2;
2 B 1. diu s c h a n d e[5] E 24 *times* (*16); 1 15 (*10); G 8
(*6); 1 B *1772; 2 B 4 (*2). diu u n é r e E l. *107; 1 7
times (*6; l. 2578, êre *with Henrici*); G *1413.

l e i d e r[6] E 6 *times*; 3764 (*MS corrupt*), 4682, 6340,
6607, 8162, 8547; 1 15; G 7; AH 6; 1 B 15; 2 B 4.

---

[1] Largely a matter of rime, the word with the greater
rime-possibilities being proportionally much more frequent in
Erec than in Iwein. For r i t t e r see Henrici on Iwein 6.

[2] Called 'unhöfisch' by Sarrazin, QuF XXXV, 12.

[3] Cf. Jaenicke p. 23; Sarrazin, QuF XXXV, 12.

[4] Again a difference in rime-facilities.

[5] s c h a d e u n d e s c h a n d e, called 'unhöfisch' by
Sarrazin QuF XXXV, 12, occurs E *3665, *4741, *7644
(zuo den schanden); for Iwein see Benecke.

[6] The corruption in Erec 3764, and the extreme rareness of
l e i d e r in Erec as compared with all the other works might
lead one to suspect the authority of the MS in this particular.

ich losche E *1780; 1 B 295, 1506. ich erlosche
E S268.

lihte (adv.) E 16 times (10 times — vielleicht, Benecke's
second division); 1 25 (17 times — vielleicht); G 7 (6 times —
vielleicht; l. 1511 against Bech); AH 7 (6 times — vielleicht;
l. 832 with Paul and Bech); 1 B 5 (3 times — vielleicht); 2
B 2 (once — vielleicht).

der lop E 24 times; I 5; G 2; AH 2; 1 B 2 (Bech also
l. 1867). der pris E 15 times(*1); I 14 (*6); G 3; AH *1;
1 B 1. der ruom[1] E 4 times (*3; *901, 1188, *4358,
*5482); G *3767; 1 B *971. lobebaere (adj.) E *1778,
*1967; G *1878. lobelich (adj.) E 7 times (*3; *323,
335, *744, 1267, *1910, 2077, 2504); I 2; AH 1420.
lobeliche (adv.) E *783, *10064. prislichen (adv.)
E 7702; I 3271.

ich loufe E 10 times (*3; l. 7001 liefen einander an —
embraced); I 19 (*2: ich loufe an (hostile); 5 times; — embrace
l. 7497); G 5 (*2). ich renne E 3 times (*1).

mich lüstet E *7354, *9310; G 2412. mich ge-
lüstet G 3395; 1 B *63.

ich mac; mahte(n)[2] E *419, *1545, *2321, *2973,
*3443, *6317, *8126, *9985, *10021; G *727. mähte E
*4522; G *1279, *1498.

daz magedin[3] E *27, *82, *1542.

---

[1] Probably a matter of accuracy of rime, or avoidance of
dialectic forms. The only other rime-word in -uom in Hartman is heiltuom (G *3768). The rimes in Erec and 1.
Büchlein are all with -uon.

[2] Haupt, on Erec 419, and Naumann, p. 34, omit
E 2973, 3443.

[3] Naumann, p. 33, seems to have overlooked E 27, in
the note on which Haupt cites the two other instances.

daz man künne. *See* künne.

m a n l i c h (*adj.*) E 8 *times* (*1); I 4; G 1; 2 B *1.
m a n l i c h e (n) (*adv.*) E *904, 2699, 6536; 1 B 722.

dax m a e r e E 35 *times* (*29; 16 *singular*, 28 *plural*);
I 45 (*39; 24 *sg.*, 21 *pl.*); G 19 (*15; 10 *sg.*, 9 *pl.*); A H *2
(*sg.*); 1 B *4 (1 *sg.*, 3 *pl.*); 2 B *1 (*pl.*).

m a e r e[1] (*adj.*) E 8 *times* (*6; l. 6374 *MS and Book
different*); I *8; G *4.

diu m a s s e n i e E 10 *times* (*5); I 1.

der m e i s t e r (— *mure*) E 7899, 7442, 7893, 8901.

diu m e n g e E 8763.   diu m e n i g i n[2] E *1699,
*9657.

der m e t e[2] E *426.

ich m i d e[4] E 10 *times* (*7; 925, 3250, *3453, *3943,
*4131, *6776, *6810, *8051, *8647, 9212); I *2; 1 B *578,
*993; 2 B 292.   ich v e r m i d e E *9 *times* (*44, *549,
*1087, *1061, *2716, *3252, *3806, *4569, *7816); I *4;
1 B *987, *1649.

m i n n e c l i c h e (n)[3] (*adv.*) E *4699, *6794; G 1144.

m i s s e v a r (*adj.*) E 3 *times* (*1; *3997, 5793, 6545);
1 B 1790; 2 B *441.

din m i s s e w e n d e E *9 *times* (âne missewende 5
times); I *1; G *2 (âne m.); A H l. *54 (âne m. L.

m i s s e z a e m e. *See* gezaeme.

ich m i s s e z i m. *See* ich gezim.

ie m i t t e n E 5 *times* (900, 6146, 6900, 6978, 8307L.

ich m u o d e E 886, 2632.

ich m u o t e (— begehre) E 4465, 4478, 5658.

m u o t v e s t e (*adj.*) E *8119; G *2098.

---

[1] See Jaenicke pp. 6 and 7 for a discussion of the various
uses of m a e r e.

[2] See statistic of rimes in -i n.

[3] Jaenicke p. 24.

[4] m i d e n and v e r m i d e n often used periphrastically.

[5] Also I. 215,2

n a m e l i c h e n (*adv.*) I *3 *times*. f ü r n a m e s (*adv.*)
I 1: AH 1359; 2 B 128, 606.

n e[1] E 224 *times*; I 565; G 173; AH 75; 1 B 62; 2 B 25.

ich n i e t e mich E 9551; G *1406.

diu n ö t. *See* arbeit.

o f t e. *See* dicke.

daz p a n z i e r E 2349, *3232.

ich p a r r i e r e E *1956, *2342, *7291.

daz p h ä r t[2] E 31 *times*; I 8; AH 1. daz r o s (ors)
E 92 *times* (*MS* ros *everywhere*, *Haupt* ors 10 *times*); I 46
(L² ors 12 *times*, *of which* 4 *have been left stand by Henrici*);
G 9 (*Paul* ors 7 *times*; *MSS differ*; E ros *in all these cases*);
A H 1 (ros).

diu p h l e g e E 13 *times* (*12; *171, *230, *2373,
*3306, *3433, *3491, 5103, *5309, *6009, *6027, *6730,
*7035, *9848); I *2; G *2278; AH *310, *1374; 2 B *570.

der p r i s. *See* lop.

p r i s l i c h e n. *See* lobeliche.

---

[1] For Erec this is, of course, entirely a matter of editing.
Bech has restored n e in many other cases, correctly so, to
judge from the above figures. Henrici's treatment differs
somewhat from L², but not sufficiently to make much difference in the figures as given. I have found some 45 cases
where he omits a n e found in L². o n w e d e r and n i e n e
have not been included in the statistic.

[2] Not found in rime in Hartman, although rimes with
ë would have been very convenient. Wolfram has 14 of these,
Walther 2, Gottfried 1 (l. 3731). See Haupt on Erec 244 for
p h ä r t used in the sense of r o s, a usage not found elsewhere in Hartman.

ich p r ü e v e[1]) E 5 *times* (1934, 3303, 5390, 7400, 7436); ich g e p r ü e v e E 5934. ich e r p r ü e v e E 7374.
der p u n e i z I 9 *times* (°1); (I °1614, °2110.
ich p u n g i e r e E °3441.

ich q u e l e E 4 *times* (6141, 6217, 6493, 6236); I B
°402.

der r a n t (*vf* schilt) E °731, 803, °3046, °9137.
diu r a s t e[2]) E °6642.
der r â t g e b e E °3934 (*M.N and Bech different*, °3904; I B 928, °1953, 1966 (*Haupt and Bech amend*), °1603; 2 B °38.

mit r e h t e (*adverbial*) E 7 *times* (°6); I 1; G 1; I B 1.
von r e h t e E 18 *times* (°3); I 6; G 1; I B 5; 2 B 2. an r e h t e E 18 *times* (°3); I 6; G 5; I B 2; 2 B 1.

ich r e i z e E 1842, °3351, 5493; G 419; AH 1157 (mich reizet); I B 448.

ich r e n n e. *See* loufe.

r i c h e (*adj.*) E 79 *times* (°30); I 23 (°10); G 24 (°7); AH 12 (°6); I B 5 (°3); 2 B 3 (°1).

r i n g e (*adj.*) E 9 *times* (°3; 1379, 4309, 4609, 6003, 6834, °7954, 8047, °8421, °8549); I °1; G 4 (°3; °122, °2504, 2834, 3698); AH 530; I B 1394. r i n g e *adv.* E 5 *times* (°3; °968, 3411, 6102, °6236, °6404); I 1; I B °679, °1872.

der r i t t e r. *See* kneht.

r i t t e r l i c h e (n) (*adv.*) E 5 *times* (°3; °1407, °1944,

___

[1]) Cf. Haupt on Erec 1954, where e r p r u e v e and g e p r ü e v o n (kunde) have, however, been confused.
[2]) Jaenicke p. 34.

*2459, 2730, 2925); (I 905 *adj. with Henrici*); G 2012, 2160.
riuwecliche(n) (*adv.*) E 9802, 9852; G 459.

daz ros. *See* phürt.

rôt (*adj.*) E 15 *times* (*4; 5 *of these of* Mâbonagrin;
l. 9317 grôz *with Haupt;* von rôtem golde l. 1445, *see Jae-nicke p. 27, who also notes l.* *7866*); I 2 (*1); G 3 (*2); 1 B
1819.

der ruom. *See* lop.

sâ[1] (*adv.*) E 27 *times* (*22; l. 5175 *with Paul, Beitr. III,
196*); I 16 (*13); G *5; AH 1; 1 B 2.

sagebaere (*adj.*) E 7570, 8372.

diu saelde[2] E 11 *times* (l. 8521 *with Bech*); I 11; G
10; AH 2; 1 B 9; 2 B 8. diu saelekeit[1] E *6 *times*
(*341, *2204, *4242, *6130, *6713, *9591); G *1235; 1 B
*3 (1219, *1343, *1361). saelic (*adj.*) E 4 *times;* I 11
(*1); G 11; AH 3; 1 B 8; 2 B 10. saeldenlôs (*adj.*)
E 3357; 1 B 1739. unsaelic (*adj.*) E 4 *times;* I 10;
G 2485; 1 B 1375.

ich salûiere E 8177, *9658.

—sam[4] (*adjectival ending*). *See Haupt on* E 214.

sam E 40 *times* (*according to Haupt; Bech has* 39, *add-ing* l. 9262, *and omitting* ll. 3085, 7081); I 16; G 5 (*Bech
alsam* l. 2191); AH 1; 1 B 4; 2 B 2. alsam E 28 *times*
(*8; *Bech and MS also* 4178); I 6 (*1); G 2 (*1); AH *524.

---

[1] For sâ zehant, sâ ze stunt see Haupt on Erec
8076, where the statement concerning Gottfried's Tristan is,
however, not entirely correct: sâ zehant occurs Tristan
1928, 11278, 11746; sâ ze stunt 931, 1136, 3696, 5346,
6259, 7778, 12219, 15312, 16194.

[2] Again a matter of rime. Cf. hoeren, kneht etc.
above.

[3] Also L *214,1.

[4] Cf. Steinmeyer, Epitheta pp. 13 and 19.

ich schaffe (strong) E 5 times (3562, 5794, 9001, 6557, 9454); I 13 (*1; especially with pronoun); G 9 (*1. 532, 502, 592, *1554, 1641, 1746, 2619, 3084, 3257; AH 904; 1 B 731, 1164, 1212; 2 B 74 (MS and Buch adopted). ich schaffe (weak) G 241, 1272, 3645; AH 770, (1 B 547 MS and Buch). ich geschaffe E 6087, 9123. I 5757; G *1476.

der schaft[1] (—sper) E 11 times (*6; 760, 761, *2610, 2803, *4726, *5513, 6923, *9067, 9086, 9112, *9115; l. *2384 — schaft); I *7102 (l. 5081 — schaft). der sper E 31 times (*14); I 21 (*11); G 8 (*3).

diu schande. See later.

diu schar[2] E 21 times (*12); I *1286. der her E 4146, *6880; I *16; G *2025, *2111; 1 B 1464.

ich schende. See unêre.

schenkel fliegen E 762, 9080; G 1890.

schiere. See balde.

schin[3] (adj.) E 96 times (*25; Buch, with MS also l. 5602; schin sin 8 times, tuon 6 times, werden 13 times; I 4 (*3; tuon 1, werden 3); G *1804 (tuon); AH *2 (werden and tuon); 1 B *5 (wesen 1, tuon 2, werden 2).

schône (adv.) E 34 times (*8); I 7 (*6); G 6 (*1); AH 1; 1 B 5 (*3); 2 B 1.

schoene (adj.) E 75 times; I 40 (*1); G 15; AH 10; 1 B 7; 2 B 4.

ich schouwe E 34 times (*23); I *11 (l. *1451 with Henrici); G *2; 2 B *2. ich beschouwe K *3 times; G *2.

[1] Called 'unhöflich' by Sarrazin, QuF XXXV, 12.
[2] Only in part due to the catalogue of knights E 1968-2117 (8 times). Cf. rimes in -ar. Also L *909,2; 311.2
[3] Cf. rimes in -in. schinen to become to become as in Erec, the figures being: E 30 times (*14); I 20 (*2); G 8 (*3); AH 1; 1 B 1. Here, however, the occurrence of the rime-pair Iwein: schein has to be taken into account (11 times). Hence also the frequency to rime to Iwein.

ich **s c h r i e** E 10 *times* (*3); I *2; G 1; AH *1; 1 B 1.

ich **s e l** G *3934; 2 B *628, *770.

s e l t e n[1] E 8 *times;* I 2; G 3; AH 2; 1 B 5 (*1); 2 B 2.

ich **s e n e** E *1880; I 9 *times* (6 *adjectival*); G 3 (*1; 2 *adjectival;* 830, 851, *1586); AH 157; 1 B *1603; 2 B 13 (*1; 9 *adjectival;* 131, *204, 239, 331, 341, 378, 404, 482, 499, 509, 568, 572, 579). **s e n l i c h** (*adj.*) I 2 *times;* 2 B 3 (208, 452, 678).

ich **s e t z e**[2] E 26 *times* (*15; gesat *14 *times:* *189, *675, *839, *1005, *1201, *1246, *3743, *4124, *6148, *6430, *7725, *7856, *8301, *9581); I 7 (*1 — gesat); G 9 (*3; gesat 3 *times:* 2646[3], *3497, *3790); AH 773; 1 B 1307, *1470 (gesat); 2 B 158.

s i d i n (*adj.*) E *1543, 8922, 10030; G 711, 1094, 1743, 1945.

ich **s i g e** E 6 *times* (*2; 222, *894, 5516, 5554, *8391, 9304); I *3943; G *120, 3123.

s i l b e r i n (*adj.*) E *190, *7690, *8956.

s i n w e l (*adj.*) E 7838, 8209, *8925.

diu **s i t e**[4] E 20 *times* (*16; *Bech and MS also* *1747, *6429, *8259); I *3 (l. 6268 *with Henrici*); G *3.

---

[1] Often used ironically, as noted by Benecke. All the Erec passages seem to come under this head, but it is impossible to distinguish sharply.

[2] The other instances in rime of a participle in -a t from **s e t z e n** are **e r s a t** E *10070; G *2170; **b e s a t** E *8681, G *918, *1846. Cf. Henrici on Iwein 2668, where the statement is slightly inaccurate and the distribution is not noted.

[3] Would be the only example outside of rime. The MSS differ and B² (changed in B³) has **g e s a m e n t**. '

[4] Explained in part by the convenience of rime with **È n i t e**. Out of the total of sixteen there are eight such rimes, aside from *1747 and *8259. Erec 9647 (**b e s i t e n**) shows the same rime. The possibility that such rimes increase the general frequency of a word in a particular work, even outside of rime, is not altogether precluded.

s l e h t (adj.) E °735x, °7343, 8448; O 2814, 2901, 2981; (2 B 206 MS and Roch).

der s m e r z e[1] E 4 times (°3231, °3430, 4409, °4894), G °8 (°810, °432, °810); AH °3 (°580, °474, °1001); 1 B °488; 2 B °478. Rimes all with herze.

s n e l[2] (adj.) (snel xe) E °1648.

diu s n e l h e i t E 3523, °3547.

s n e l l e. See balde.

s n ê v a r. See wiz.

s n ê w i z. See wiz.

s p a e h e (adj.) E °1997, °7643; 1 °8941.

s p a e h e (adv.) AH 1411.

diu s p a e h e E 7 times (°6; °3103, °6772, 6779, °8135, °8349, °9449, °10097).

das s p e r. See schaft.

der s p i l m a n E °2138, °2190.

s t a r k e (adv.) E °2176, °7416, 7508; 1 18 times; G[3] 9 (°6; °956, °1100, 1118, °1149, °1914, 1992, 1633, °1765, °2264); AH 845; 2 B 149.

diu s t a t[4] E 37 times (°24); 1 16 (°10); G 16 (°10); AH 1; 1 B 1.

s t a e t e[5] (adj.) E 17 times (°8); 1 4; O 6 (°3); AH 4 (°2); 1 B 4 (°1); 2 B 5.   u n s t a e t e (adj.) E °3 times; 1 °1; 1 B °2.   diu s t a e t e E 6 times (°2); 1 °2; O °3; AH 2;

---

[1] Cf. Erich Schmidt QuF IV, 106-8 and Bech QuF XXXIII, 52. English parallel s m a r t and h e a r t.

[2] Jaenicke p. 11.

[3] As the number of instances in rime itself would indicate, this is due to the rime-pairs b a r k e : s t a r k e (twice) and m a r k e : s t a r k e (five times).

[4] Cf. s e t z e above. It is possible to argue that g e s a t is less common in Iwein simply because s t a t is, but this is sufficiently controverted by a comparison of the rime-pair b a t : s t a t (E 11 times, 1 7) with g e s a t : s t a t (E 9 times, 1 1).

[5] See h â t e, h a e t e in the discussion of rime.

1 B *2; 2 B 5. diu staetekeit[1] E *8144; 2 B *327. diu unstaete E *2 times; I 2; 1 B *2.

ich strite[1] E *6 times; 1 21 (*17); G *2; 2 B *1. ich gestrite E *3 times; I *3; 1 B *1; 2 B *1. ich vihte E 18 (*4); I 27 (including daz vehten; *7). ich gevihte I *1.

diu stunde E *38 times (23 sg., 10 pl.[3]); I *19 (5 sg., 14 pl.); G *17 (14 sg., 3 pl.); AH *4 (3 sg., 1 pl.); 1 B *2 (sg.); 2 B *1 (sg.).

sum[4] (adj.) E *7635. sumelich E 4220.

der surzengel E 820, 2798; G 1604.

sus[5] (adv.) E 54 times (*3); I 59; G 39 (*5 — grêgôrjus: sus); A H 14; 1 B 4; 2 B 4. Cf. alsus.

swach (adj.) E 12 times (359, 580, 1587, 2184, 2800, 2849, 4202, 5783, 6476. 6487, 8123, 8289); I 5; G 520, 2949, 3039; AH 1332ᵇ; 1 B 5 (245, 798, 1079, 1103, 1232).

diu swaere. See arbeit.

ich swige. See dage.

diu tât I *2 times.

ich tobe I 6 times (*2); G 3307; 1 B *1513; 2 B 229. Cf. wüete.

diu tôrheit E *6519; G 2789; 2 B 229. toerlich (adj.) E *9030. toerlîche (adv.) E 6532, 7010, 9005.

ich touc. See gezim.

---

[1] Also L *206,₁₇; 211,₃₈. unstaetekeit L *211,₁₇.

[2] Cf. justieren.

[3] Doubtful forms are classed as singular. Compare ze stunt etc. The Gregorius statistic includes three cases of ze stunde.

[4] Cf. Haupt on Erec 7635. sumelich also L 212,₂₄.

[5] Cf. Sievers, PBB XII, 498. AH 410 seems, however, to be another clear exception to the rule, and sus is there not in rime, as it is in Gregorius 1285.

— 35 —

der trehtîn E °1963 (: küneginne) 1 °3 (, ...

ich trâwe E 4 times (1404, 1461, ...) 1 1
(l. 4101 ge- with Henrici); G 73, 1476; AH 139, 1 B ...
ich getrâwe E 6101; 1 3 times; U 6, °3; 107, °804, ...
1727, °2659, 2898); AH 663, 1159; 1 B °37, 2 B 570.

tugenthaft (adj.) E 15 times (961, 1094, 1702, ...
2784, 2811, 2876, 2798, 4066, 4442, 4738, 4817, ...
7842); 1 B 1499. tugentriche (adj.) E 6 times, °3,
°1806, °4494, 5713, °5988, °6784, °8110. tugent-
liche(n) (adv.) E 3 times (°1; 4646, °3668, 5894). AH
1889.

diu tuht E °995, 2587.

tump (adj.) E 11 times (°6); 1 4; U 5; AH 4, 1 B 2,
2 B °1.

ich überkume 1 °3 times; G °9177. ich über-
winde E 10 times (°5); 1 18 (°15); U °2; 1 B °3; 2 B °2.
ich überlade 1 °4 times; G °404, °1669; 2 B °78.
unbewart (adj.) E °6875; U °2194.
unbiderbe. See biderbe.
unbillich (adj.) 1 2 (°1); 2 B °768.
undaere (adj.) 1 B °1710. undâre (adv.) 1 908?.
1 B °1418.
unde (temp. rel.) E 7026 (see Haupt), 4608.
diu unêre. See êre.
ich unêre 1 10 times (°7). ich entêre 1 °1 ich
schende E °2190 (geschant), °3641; 1 4668; U °1864,
°3810.
unerkant (adj.) E °2 times; 1 °1; 1 B °1. 2 B °1
unkunt E 7 times (°5); 1 °3; U 3 (°1); AH °1; 1 B °1
unervaeret (adj.) E °2773; 1 °2 times unver-
vorht (adj.) 1 °2 times. unversagt (adj.) E 7 times
(°2; °4306, 4430, 5557, °6694, 8131, 9171, 6665). 1 B (°1.
unzagehaft (adj.) E °9177.

u n g e l i c h e. *See* geliche.

u n g e m a c h[1] *(adj.)* E *7 *times* (*690, *1079, *4049, *4263, *5477, *6538, *7823); I *4.

daz u n g e v a l E *6034. daz u n g e v e l l e I *3 *times.*

diu u n g e f u o g e. *See* unsite.

u n g e z a e m e. *See* gezaeme.

u n k u n t. *See* unerkant.

u n m a e r e *(adj.)* E *4456; I 9 *times* (*8); G *4 (*970, *1914, *2944, *3037); AH *126; I B *3 (*164, *1608, *1728).

u n m ü g e l i c h *(adj.)* I *5 *times;* G *2; AH *4.

u n s æ l i c. *See* sælic.

der u n s i t e I 3(*2);G 1298, *3086. diu u n g e f u o g e E *6528, *9518. diu u n f u o g e E *5472; I 860. diu u n f u o r e E 1244.

u n s t æ t e. *See* stæte.

u n v e r z a g t. *See* unervaeret.

u n f r u o t. *See* fruot.

diu u n f u o g e. *See* unsite.

diu u n f u o r e. *See* unsite.

u n z a g e h a f t. *See* unervaeret.

diu u n z i t E *1226, *8841.

u p p i c *(adj.)* AH 86; I B 519, 804, 1176. diu u p p e k e i t I B 722.

daz u r l i u g e[2] E 408; G 910, 1874, 1898.

der v â l a n t E *4 *times* (*5556, *5648, *9197, *9270); I B *1683.

---

[1] Haupt on Erec 2271 seems to know of only one instance (4263) in Erec It might be possible to conceive of some of the above as substantives, but this seems forced, and they do not differ from the Iwein examples.

[2] Jaenicke p. 18.

der valsch[1] N n times (1302, 6642, 6651, 6682, 6692, 7588, 8587, 9488); AH 51; 1 N 3 (804, 844, 1042, 1641, 1757); 2 B 997. diu valscheit E °2724, 1 *g times

diu varwe[2] K 34 times (34 counting 1 5692, and E[0] and Book: °10); 11; G 3 (°9): AH 1120; 1 B °796. an anndervarwe E °7396.

veige[3] (adj.) 1 1209.

ich verbiude. See binde.

daz verch[4] 1 3 times. verchwoni (adj.) K 6682 diu verchwunde G °140.

ich verdenke 1 4 times.

ich verdiene E 9678 (passage interpolated according to Pfeiffer): 1 7 times (3 of them, 1302, 7781, 7900 changed to godiene by Henrici): G 3543; AH 1420; 1 B 146, 784 and gediene E 8 times (987, 1374, 1949, 4640, 5624, 5687, 6569, 7782); 13 times (6 according to Henrici; G 1716, 1984; AH 288, 884; 1 B 264, 800, 1664; 3 B 76, 182 and verschulde E 4960, 4991, 6708; 1 3 times; 6 9612, 2691. ich versol E °3562, °2927, °6463; 1 N 24, °822

vergeben(e) E 4239, 9944; 1 B 429.

ich vernim. See hoere.

ich versage E °4072, °2648; 1 11 times (°6; G °1133, °1702, °1708; AH °238; 1 B °512, 1641

ich verschulde. See verdiene.

ich versêre E °4727; 1 B °487.

ich versihe mich E 2497; 1 7 times (°34, 6 9260, AH °969, °1103; 1 B °1255; 2 B °13

ich versol. See verdiene.

ich verswache E 1763, 4658, 4742, 6292.

---

1) Also I. 211, 4; 213.n.
2) The rimes are all with garwe and its compounds.
3) Jaenicke p. 12.
4) See Jaenicke p. 24, who does not mention verchwoni and verchwunde, although in both the first passages verch is joined with wunde. Henrici reads verre I 7785; see Paul on the passage.

ich verwize. *See* wize.

ich verzage E 6 *times* (*3): I 13 (*9); G 2 (*1); AH *4; 1 B *8; 2 B *1.

rient. *See* gelinz.

vil. *See* harte.

viurin (*adj.*) E 882, *9206.

der vliz[1] E 23 *times* (*18); I 4; G 7 (*3); 2 B 2 (*1).

ich vlize mich E 8 *times* (*2); I 2 (*1); G 4 (*2); 1 B 4 (*1).

vol (*adj.*) E 24 *times* (*9; l. 2050 wol *with MS and Bech*); I 8 (*3); G 8 (*3); AH 4 (*1); 1 B 1.

vollecliche (n) (*adv.*) E 13 *times* (*4); I 5 (*1); G 3; AH *1.

diu freise E 7 *times* (*4; *146, *3136, *6871, *7947, 7954, 8059, 8818); I 2; G *4 (*775, *954, *1036, *3367); 1 B 191. enfreise (*adv.*) E *6097. diu wegefreise G *3748. freislich (*adj.*) E 5399.

ich freue. *See* frô.

vrevel(e)[2] (*adj.*) I 1; G 250, 3868. vrevellich (*adj.*) I 1; G 3800. vrevelliche (*adv.*) G 102. diu vrevele G 1995.

diu frist E *9 *times;* I *17; G *6; AH *3; 1 B *2; 2 B *2. diu wile E 22 *times* (*9); I 17 (*2); G 3; AH 1; 1 B 7; 2 B *1. diu zit[3] E 65 *times* (*52; l. 9485 *with MS and Bech*); I 37 (*24); G 15 (*8); AH 3 (*2); 1 B *7; 2 B 6 (*3).

diu friundin[4] (-inne) E 14 (*12); I 1303 (*Henrici* vriunt).

---

[1] Cf. wiz. Eleven of the eighteen rimes in Erec are with forms of wiz. Of those remaining four are with foreign words in -i z.

[2] Jaenicke pp. 15 and 16.

[3] In Erec 11 times in rime with Ênite.

[4] See discussion of rimes in -in. Of the above Erec shows 10 (*9) -in and 4 (*3) -inne forms.

friuntlich (adj.) E 7 times; 1 2; 2 B 1 freuntliche(n) (adv.) E 5 times (*2); 1 1; G 1.

frô (adj.) E 47 times (*45) 1 34 (*31); G 16 (*18; AH 4 (*3); 1 B 4 (*6); 2 B *2. ich frewe E 7 times; 1 14 (*1); G 2; AH 4; 1 B 2; 2 B 2. ich gefrewe 1 *1.

frum (adj.) E 12 times; 1 17; G 8; AH 5; 2 B 2 cf. biderbe. diu frumcheit E 18 times (*7); 1 10 (*14; II. 4561 and 6944 om. in Henrici); G 4 (*1); 1 B *1.

diu frume, der frume E 4101; 17 times; 1 B 521, 1533; 2 B 590, 642.

fruot (adj.) 1 B *1242; 2 N *174, 104, *214 so fruot 1 B *249, *549.

ich fliege E 5 (*1; 1060, 2427, *4451, 6724, 6920, 1 12 times (*2; 1 *7254 with Henrici). G 1900; 1 B 5174 ich geflege E 490, 561; 14 times (*1); G 1024, 1 B *24, *665, *727, *769.

das fürbliege E *590, 2797, *7781, 7751.

fürnamen. See namelichen.

diu wal E 3 times (*2; 8905, *2968, *7791; G 6 (*7, 1489, *2086, *2793, *2261, 8717, *3184; 1 B *1468, 2 B 112.

ich walte E *11 times (*314, *234, *1422, *1922, *2664, *3956, *7016, *7205, *5544, *5567, *5608; 1 *5542, G *5 (*217, *567, *745, *2712, *7489); 1 B 1, *10454.

der wân E 31 times (*30); 1 18 (*11; G *2, AH *3; 1 B 7 (*6); 2 B *2.

ich wandel E 2984, 6942; 1 B 594, 1944.

wanne(n) (*adv.*) E (4187 *MS and Bech*), 5155, 9336; G 1224, 1227, 1805, 1861, 2571.

ich **wâpen** mich E 3064.

der **wâpenroc** E 6 *times* (740, 2339, 2568, 4482, 4487, 9018).

diu **wât.** *See* gewant.

der **wec**[1] E 69 *times* (*48; l. 7814 *with MS and Bech*); I 27 (*8); G 13 (*9); AH 4 (*2); 1 B 3 (*1); 2 B *1.

weizgot[1] E 1355, 4743, 8948; I 9 *times;* G 8 (872, 1804, 1415, 1501, 2416, 2592, 2941, 3116); AH 925; 1 B 75, 207, 583.

daz **werc** E 6 *times:* I 11 (*1); G 2; 1 B 5.

diu **werdekeit** E *6 *times* (*377, *2068, *2438, *4629, *5085, *7860); AH *89, *117. **wirdecliche** (*adv.*) E *5094, *9993.

diu **werltminne** 1 B *1426. diu **werltsache** E *7252. der **werlttôre** AH 396. daz **werltwip** 2 B *630. der **werltwise** (man) E 7368. diu **werltwünne** 1 B 277, 1856. der **werltzage** E *4657; AH *1320.

wert[3] (*adj.*) E 10 *times* (*6; *3779, *4709, *4950, 5258, *6472, *6931, 7195, 8188, *9307, 9352); I 15 (*10); G 4 (*2: *869, 1894, 2897, *3501); AH *761; 1 B 5 (*4: *234, *787, *1461, *1471, 1479); 2 B *444, *782.

der **widergelt** E 877, 5642, *5750.

ich **widerrite** E *1239, *3118, *8023.

ich **widersage** I 9 *times* (*8); G *2724, *2747; 1 B *766.

der **widerslac** I 2 *times* (*1).

---

[1] Illustrates very well the influence of rime on diction: the rime pair **Erec**: **wec** occurs 31 times in Erec.

[2] Schönbach p. 4 ff.

[3] Cf. Steinmeyer, Epitheta pp. 9 and 18 (Note 18), where, however, G 1894 should be added for Hartman, possibly also E *6931, *9307 (**der werde**), and 2 B 782 (**diu werde**); G *3501 has **der gotes werde.**

— 33 —

der widerstrit E °3 times (°8702, °8703, ..., °7801, °8733).

widerzaume. See ......

diu wile. See frist.

wiplich(e)n (adv.) E 6 times (°1, 581, ..., ..., °5107, 5918, 6234).

wirdecliche. See ....

der. din wis E 1716, 3431; I 7 times (°11; U 4 (1884, 2028, 3337, 3483); 1 B 112, 1773; 2 B °166, ...).

wiselôs (adj.) E °230, °6180; U 6332, 5770; 1 B 1582.

wiz (adj.) E 20 times (°3); 11; G °1; 2 B 1. endels (adj.) E °276, °2030. enôrar E °3081. Cf. .... die wize E 7307; G °3431; 2 B °143.

ich wize E 6304, 6399 (MS and Buch ver.., ... (MS and Buch ver.); 1 B 549, 587; (MS and Buch ver.); 2 B 15. ich verwize E °321, 3766, 4961; 1 B 201

ich won o¹) (— wohne) E 5191, 5474; 1 7 times; U ..., 343, °561, 2366, 2560; AII 327, 504; 1 B ...., °1343; 2 B °735.

daz wortzeichen E °1895, 5964; G 3417

ich whete E °859, °3598. Cf. ....

mich nimt wunder E 7 times (°4, ..., ..., ..., °3730, °4849, °4938, 5803); G °1480; AII °1071; 1 B ...., mich wundert E 18 times (14, 2839, 3136, 5464, ..., 6601, 6649, 7932, 7940, 8701, 5771, 9183; 1 6; G ...., 1625, 2631; AII 377; 1 B 1392.

wunneclich (adj.) E 16 times (°3; 1787, °3511, 5739, 6193, 6316, °7918, ..., 8333, 8992, 9710, °....., 9933, 9417, °9474, 9545, 9775); 1 3 °11; G 674, ... AII °1273. wunnecliche(n)²) (adv.) E 6316, ...; G °204, 915; 2 B 63.

---

¹) In Erec in the literal sense; all the other cases, with the exception of G °561, are used more or less figuratively.

²) Also L 211.w.

der wunsch E 14 *times* (332, 1700, 2207, 2741,
5964, 6487, 7181, 7378, 7796, 7842, 8214, 8222, 8935, 10115;
I 5: G 5 (1263, 1969, 1458, 2261, 3389); AH 56; 2 B 113.
daz wunschkint E *8278. daz wunschleben I *1:
AH *393; 2 B *79. daz wunschspil E *8530. der
wunschwint G *787.

daz zabel G 2029, 2031. der zabelaere E 943.
zagehaft (*adj.*) I 2 *times* (*1); 2 B 549. zagelich
(*adj.*) E 8630. zagelichen (*adv.*) E *6882.

diu zal[1] E 11 *times* (*10; *281, *1389, *1696, *1941,
*3567, *4043, 6807, *6854, *7780, *7835, *7862); I *1: 1 B
*1050.

ich zal. *See* zel.

ich ze(r)briche E 22 *times* (*15); I *8; G 2 (*1);
AH 4 (*3); 2 B *1. ich gebriche I *1; AH *1. ich
briche E 13 *times* (*11): I 16 (*9); G 7 (*4): AH 6 (*4):
1 B *2; 2 B *1.

zehant (*adv.*) E 34 *times* (*22); I 32 (*22); G 11 (*9);
AH 5 (*4); 1 B 1; 2 B 1. ze hant E 5 *times* (*2); G *1.
alzehant AH *1190. zestunt E *9 *times* (*755,
*1163, *3088, *3098, *3209, *3424, *4237, *5223, *8103):
I *3; G *448, *3783, *3860; AH *1180, *1369; 1 B *1821.
ze stunt E *6 *times* (*2881, *3349, *4833, *6771, *6847,
*6932): G *548. ze stunde[2] E *9 *times* (*4943, *5124,
*5293, *6073, *8157, *9003, *9615, *9624, *9666); G (ze
munde) *1210, *2878, *3726.

ich zel, zal E *20 *times* (er zalt *743, *1625, *1942,
*5218; gezalt *1939, *2921, *5655, *5704, *6127, *6767,
*7339, *7429, *7461, *8376, *8624: zellen *2079, *2233,
*2828, *7457; zeln *1403); I 836 (zelt): G (gezalt) 3465,
*3676; 1 B 8 (*5; zel mir 741; zaltest 83; zalen *450; zelen

---

[1] zal: über al 5 times in Erec, once in Iwein.
[2] Cf. stunde.

674; gewalt °632, °1322, °1500, °1533µ; 2 B °013 unten.
ich überzal I °5007.

mir zerinnet E 6 times (°4; °6n4, 1261, 2152,
°2492, °9256, °9761); I °1; 1 B °410, °1724, °1004;
2 B °17.

zesam(e)ne (adv.) E 90 times; schieben 766, 612,
2605, 9064; binden 1572, 2544, 3406, 4045, tragen 214,
9186; senden 9105, 9749; geparieret 1956, 2248; rion
4207, 4882; gân lân 632, 6912; — 612, 614, 1706, 2122,
2793, 7544, 7851, 7856, 9120, (9344 XI and Benb, 9724,
9856; I 6 times; G 2 (2122, 2175, 2195); 1 B 4 (434, 544,
1390, 1538).

zestunt. See mahant.
ich ziere E 14 times (°10; °737, °1957, 2394, °2244,
°2434, °2800, °4687, °7990, 7842, °7945, °7994, 4624,
3304, °9659); I °2554; G 722, 575; (1 B 1400 XI and Benb.

daz zil E 12 times (°11; ich nim mir des als ich °2904,
°6047, °6576, °8588; °871, °2454, 2974, °5417, °6571,
°6385, °8715, °9554); I °5; G °342, 549, °1047, °1291;
AH °607; 1 B °1028, °1476, °1544.

ich zim. See gezim.
ziph (interj.) 1 B 817.
diu zit. See frist.
der zobel E 9000, 9010, 9017; AH 1055. gezobelt
E 1572, 1999, 8944. zobelin (adj.) E °9904.

diu zunge I 5 times; G °2, °9006; AH 642, 669;
1 B 818.

zwâre (adv.). See deiswâr.

RIME-TECHNIC.

The subject will be treated under the following heads:
1. Rime-vowels. 2. Rime-groups. 3. Identical Rime ('rüh-render reim'). 4. Impure rimes.

The results of an examination of the vowels employed in rime in the different works of Hartman are largely negative. The following table presents the sum-totals for each vowel and the relative percentage of each. These totals refer to couplets, not lines. The 'Leich' of the Erstes Büchlein is not included in the statistic.

	E	I	G	AH	1 B	2 B
a	1392	1030	518	131	133	71
	27.466	25.227	25.861	17.124	16.18	17.191
à	460	343	172	56	84	34
	9.077	8.401	8.587	7.32	10.219	8.232
ae	160	109	101	19	29	8
	3.157	2.67	5.042	2.484	3.528	1.937
e	540	417	187	98	65	43
	10.655	10.213	9.336	12.81	7.908	10.412
è	117	151	69	19	43	22
	2.309	3.698	3.445	2.484	5.231	5.327
ei	300	325	132	51	47	33
	5.919	7.96	6.59	6.667	5.718	7.99

876	493	194	104	124	90
7.459	11.952	0.126	12.856	16.846	14.044
550	936	109	43	67	
10.852	8.27	5.049	6.691	6.151	8.644
171	100	54	14	19	6
8.874	7.449	3.494	3.243	2.511	1.463
278	253	133	66	60	
5.887	6.196	6.74	6.018	7.176	
3	7	3	4	0	1
.059	.171	.15	.363	0	.348
181	144	75	51	36	37
8.571	3.897	3.744	4.447		
9	3	1	9	1	1
.039	.133	.05	.361	.133	
54	16	13	n	8	9
1.065	.392	.649	1.046	.73	.464
0	8	1	0	6	0
0	.196	.05	0	0	0
157	141	63	33	19	18
3.093	3.453	4.164	4.372	3.211	3.146
19	16	23	7	8	8
.387	.392	1.148	.916	.600	.464
25	34	10	3	4	1
.493	.343	.490	.399	.457	.343
41	25	20	10	4	9
.809	.612	.999	1.307	.457	.464
231	300	102	47	70	90
4.555	4.896	5.092	6.144	6.510	7.904
21	25	14	13	7	1
.414	.612	.699	1.699	.345	.343

To show the variation possible within the limits of one and the same poem the following statistics for each 1000 lines of Iwein are appended.

	1-1000	-2000	-3000	-4000	-5000	-6000	-7000	-8000
a	132	187	127	138	105	121	124	130
â	42	32	42	35	52	38	52	43
ae	15	15	11	18	12	20	11	6
e	36	46	54	43	63	50	58	54
ê	18	14	22	15	22	16	20	22
ei	48	37	40	41	35	33	39	44
i	61	68	44	47	68	57	63	68
î	37	25	38	39	37	31	28	15
ie	13	9	9	19	12	13	10	14
o	30	35	35	19	31	34	34	30
ö	1	3	0	0	0	1	1	1
ô	17	14	16	19	18	20	16	22
oe	1	0	1	0	1	0	1	1
ou	3	3	1	3	1	3	2	0
ou	1	0	0	0	0	2	5	0
u	16	16	16	21	17	16	15	19
ü	1	6	0	3	2	0	1	3
û	3	1	6	4	4	3	2	1
iu	4	4	3	5	2	2	2	3
uo	19	28	31	29	18	38	12	20
üe	2	7	4	2	0	2	4	4

It will be seen from the above table that the extremes are: for a 105–138; â 32–52; ae 6–20; e 36–63; ê 14–22; ei 33–48; i 44–68; î 15–39; ie 9–19; o 19–35; ö 0–3; ô 14–22; oe 0–1; ou 0–3; ou 0–5; u 15–21; ü 0–6; û 1–6; iu 2–5; uo 12–38; üe 0–7.

Examining these results, it is found that ten vowels and diphthongs, â, e, ei, ie, o, ö, ou, ü, û, uo, show greater variation in these divisions of 1000 lines from Iwein, than they do in the six poems each taken as a whole; on the other hand, eleven vowels and diphthongs, a, ae, ê, i, î, ô, oe, ou, u, iu,

to show less variation in the ~~second table than in the first~~.
These latter are as rime-vowels ~~numerically the stronger~~,
representing in the case of Irwin 53.3 per cent of the rime
stock as over against 41.5 per cent ~~belonging to the first group~~.

By a close scrutiny of the rime-work of each ~~particular~~
poem, it would be possible to discover in each ~~instance~~ the
elements that go to make up this ~~difference~~ in the ~~relative~~
percentages of rime-vowels. Thus the low ~~average of the~~
1 and 2 Büchlein for *a* is due to the ~~scarcity or total absence of~~
such rime-words as: lac, pflac, brach, ~~nach, ge~~-
schach, sprach, nam, quam, lant, ~~mostly words~~
that belong to narrative rather than ~~reflective poetry~~. One
might thus go through the rimes of each poem, ~~specifying the~~
particular words that are abnormal in their ~~ratio of frequency~~.
Though involving less detail, something ~~similar will be at~~-
tempted in the discussion of rime-groups. The ~~subsequent~~
publication of a complete rime-index will, ~~it is hoped, supple~~-
ment this latter work.

It was said at the outset that the result of this ~~examination~~
of rime-vowels would be largely negative. This may, in the
case of Hartman, be partly due to the fact that his ~~works deal~~
with widely-varying subjects and that ~~hence both word-stock~~
and rime-stock show great variations. In any case it ~~cannot~~
be denied that the latter goes hand in hand with the ~~former~~,
and that the only strictly scientific method of ~~investigation is to~~
examine the two together. Even such externals as the ~~names~~
of persons playing important parts in a poem may ~~exert great~~
influence on the sum-total of certain rime-vowels.

If of little use in determining chronology, ~~estimates of~~
rime-vowels seem of still more doubtful value in ~~determining~~
authorship. While not disputing the ~~correctness of Stein~~-
meyer's conclusion in GGA 1843, pp. 124 ~~f, the method there~~
employed seems open to criticism. To test its ~~soundness, it is~~
only necessary to apply the same method to the four ~~epics of~~
Hartman: Erec, Iwein, Gregorius and Der arme Heinrich.
The results would be (Steinmeyer classes all *a*, ~~ä, ö~~ ... and *o*

vowels together): *a* E .397, G.394, I .363, AH .269; *e* AH
.22, I .219, G .194, E .189; *i* E .217, AH .216, I .207,
G .172; *o* AH .145, G .114, I .106, E .101; *u* AH .15,
G .126, I .106, E .096. It will be seen that in this comparison Der arme Heinrich is quite as abnormal as Mai und
Beaflor in Steinmeyer's statistics. To a large extent such
variations are a mere reflex of the diction, and differences in
the latter are as often due to subject and period of production
as to authorship. In any case it is safer to base conclusions
on an examination of particular rime-groups than on the statistic
of rime-vowels, as by this method we come nearer to diction
proper, the ultimate basis on which the whole matter rests.
Steinmeyer has examined fifteen different groups to show the
variation in Mai und Beaflor and here his evidence seems more
convincing than it did in the case of rime-vowels. I now
propose to attempt something similar, on a more extensive
scale, for Hartman.

RIME-GROUPS.

Part of the material has already been given under the
head of 'Diction', where occurrences in rime have consistently
been separated from those in the middle of the line. As a rule,
phenomena suggested by an examination of the dictionary
proper have found a place under 'Diction', while those suggested by a study of the rime-index have been grouped under
the present head. The arrangement is alphabetic, according
to that usually employed in rime-indices, although differing in
some details. The groups selected are mainly such of the
larger ones as show considerable divergence of usage. As a
rule the smaller groups have been given only when of especial
interest. Statistics of particular rime-couplets or rime-words,
properly subdivisions of those for rime-endings, have usually
been relegated to the foot notes; where not, they are enclosed
in brackets. Identical and impure rimes, being treated under
separate heads, have not been regularly noted. The 'Leich' of
the Erstes Buchlein is not included in the statistic.

(verdagest: sagest[1] 1 B 1391; 1480, ager
E 14; G 8; AH 15; 1 B 1. agt[1] E 10; 1 81, G 6, AH 3,
1 B 1. ahrt[1] E 15; 19; G 7; 1 B 1; 2 B 1. abler E 19.
11; G 1; AH 1; 1 B 1. ablet E 3. ar E 83. 19.
G 7; 1 B 1. alt[1] E 31; 1 13; G 7; AH 9; 1 Be; 9 B 1
alt[1] E 9; 11; G 9; 2 B 1. alten[1] E 11, 1 8; G 11;
1 B 1; 2 B 2. am[1] E 79; 1 19; G 19; AH 9. 1 B 1.

---

[1] The reading of a g e t or a g t is largely a matter of
editing. Henrici and I, are, however, in exact agreement the
Iwein. Of forms that also show contraction into o i, there
are, aside from s a g e s t above: s a g e t (3 p. sg., including
cpds.) E 1257, 1587; G 2447; AH 301; 1 B 340. g e s a g e t
(participle; cpds.) E 1103, 2711, 6305, 7033, 7131. 6573, 14
2841, 2576; AH 223, 356, 445, 459, 554, 708, 971, 1040,
1113, 1493. s a g t (3 p. sg., with cpds.) E 1417, 1090,
10039; 1 840, 6575; G 2296, 3890; 1 B 340. g e s a g t
(part., cpds.) E 311, 2812, 5109, 6421; 1 328, 730, 1304,
1622, 1742, 1757, 1820, 2088, 3534, 4473, 5903, 5700, 6430,
6565, 6594, 7286, 7656; G 1428, 1760. s a g t e (cpds.) E
4839, 8307, 8464; 1 952, 3693; G 1703, 2347, 7293. AH
583. All of these are coupled with rime-words that never
show o i - forms. These figures differ somewhat from Fischer's
Zur Geschichte des Mittelhochdeutschen p. 46. Compare the
statistics below of rimes in o i s t, e i t and e i t e.

[2] Of past participles from verbs in -e c k e n there are
b e d a h t E 1851, 2145, 7382, 8773 (:gestaht); 1 601,
7518; G 354, 934, 2489; u n b e d a h t K 1700, 6096,
b e s t a h t E 2876; g e s t a h t E 8773 (:bedaht or
w a h t (:naht) AH 541. For e i w a h t see also rime
in e c k e t.

[3] See m a c, p. 24. Cf. m o h t e (n) below.

[4] See z a l under Diction. Forms of a l (adj.) in rime
E 38; 1 17; G 10; AH 9; 1 B 2.

[5] Cf. ich z e l p. 40. No doublets of participles in
-a l t and -e l l e t occur.

[6] Preterit forms: s t a l t e E 7342, g e v a l t e E 3467.

[7] Cf. ich w a l t e p. 37.

[8] See also rimes in a e m e below. Largely preterits of
n e m e n, k o m e n and z e m e n, with these compounds
n a m (and cpds.) in rime E 60; 1 10; G 16; AH 9; 1 B 1.
q u a m (and cpds.) E 55; 1 7; G 11; AH 1; g e n a m and
z a m E 26; 1 2; G 3. n a m : q u a m (with these cpds.

a n[1] E 223; I 187; G 95; AH 9; 1 B 32; 2 B 22. a n d e[2] E 31; I 15; G 15; AH 2; 2 B 2. a n t[3] E 164; I 120; G 57; AH 16; 1 B 4; 2 B 3. a r[4] E 67; I 42; G 20; AH 5; 1 B 6; 2 B 5. (was E 30; I 15; G 19; AH 3.) a t[5] E 30; I 11; G 15; AH 1; 1 B 1. (b a t e r : v a t e r E 1466, 1820; G 2287; AH 567, 641. 961.) (s a z z e r : w a z z e r E 6716).

E 42; I 7; G 10; AH 1. For g e z a m see g e z i m under Diction. n e m e n (v e r-, g e-, b e-) altogether is found: E 272 times; I 150; G 80; AH 24; 1 B 42; 2 B 15. k o m e n (b e-) altogether, E 232; I 162; G 61; AH 18; 1 B 24; 2 B 11. The phenomenon is probably explained by reference to k o m, the other, regular form of the preterit, which has no rime-facilities, and is used only inside the line. If the above statistic is held to show that the *a* form is used only for the sake of rime, it is probably to be confined to that position even in Erec. Compare q u â m e n below.

[1] Among the rime-paire are: b e g a n : m a n E 15; I 4; 1 B 1; k a n : m a n E 18; I 26; G 8; AH 1; 1 B 5; 2 B 8; m a n : g e w a n E 49; I 23; G 11; AH 1; 1 B 5; 2 B 3. For b e g a n : m a n see b e g i n n e under Diction. Total number of occurrences of g e w i n n e n in Hartman: E 93; I 79; G 34; AH 10; 1 B 26; 2 B 5. i e m a n and n i e m a n in rime as follows (in accordance with which Henrici on Iwein 194 may be corrected): n i e m a n : a n E 4771; : d a n E 1481, 2663; I 1268, 3228; : k a n E 8254; I 5890; AH 443; : g e w a n G 1246; i e m a n : g e w a n E 423; I 2826. For i e m e n and n i e m e n in rime see below.

[2] s a n d e (and cpds.) E 1893, 2879, 4920, 6117 (: e r- w a n d e), 7566 (: e r w a n d e), 10055; G 194, 718, 937, 942, 2509; also Leich 1764, 1766. w a n d e (e r-) E 6116, 6667, 7567; also L 215,17. s a n t e (: e r m a n t e) G 2852; w a n t e n (: l a n t e n) G 1849 (MSS differ). The forms in *t* had few rime-facilities. Apparently the *d*-forms are not found in rime after Erec, Erstes Büchlein and Gregorius. This would make L 215,14 early also.

[3] z e h a n t : v a n t I 11; G 4; AH 2. l a n t : g e n a n t E 12; I 2; G 2. Participles in -a n t that also show forms in -e n d e t : g e w a n t (and cpds.) E 16; I 19; G 8; AH 3; 1 B 1. g e s c h a n t E 2190 (emend. of Lachmann). For e n d e t-forms see below. Cf. Lachmann on I 7967.

[4] Cf. s c h a r p. 29. Statistic for g a r : E 100 (*44); I 70 (*21); G 28 (*10); AH 15 (*3); 1 B 25 (*4); 2 B 13 (*4).

[5] Cf. i c h s e t z e p. 30.

ä[1] E 46; I 25; G 9; AH 1.   âht K 11; I 4; G 2.
AH 3; 1 B 3.   âhte E 8; I 2; G 1; AH 1.   qebwer
E 2; G 5.)   ân[2] E 199; I 158; G 34; AH 99; 1 B 23; 2 B
14.   (begânt:hânt E 6386(MSdif.); enhânt·et Ânt
E 8100 (MSdif.); lânt:stânt I 509).   âre[3] E 1; I 9; G 4;
1 B 1.   (bâst E 2; I 1; AH 4; 1 B 4.   âr[4] E 62; I 80;

---

[1] dâ in rime E 38; I 19; G 7; AH 1.   CN ed p 99.

[2] E 662, 7718; G 629, 1979, 3195, 3375, 3732.   See
note on am; there are no rimes in -ô m e n.

[3] hân (1 ps. sg., 1 p. pl., inf.): lâ n daf., past part.
E 6; I 16; G 1; AH 1; 1 B 3.   hân daf., 1 ps. sg.; wâ e
E 10; I 2; G 1; AH 1; 1 B 3; 2 B 1.   Infinitive gâ e and
cpds.) in rime E 35; I 26; G 9; AH 5; 1 B 7; 2 B 6; past
part. -gân E 2706 (MS diff.), 9652, 5719 (MS diff.), 9633;
I 3694; (past part. -gangen E 12 times; I 17; G 4;
other forms in ân: 1 ps. sg. E 4963; G 2573; 1 ps. pl. E
909.   For ên see below.   Infin. hân in rime E 41; I 80;
G 8; AH 6; 1 B 4; 2 B 3; (inf. haben E 7544, 7545
subst.; I 1965, 5965.)   1 ps. sg. hân E 28; I 82; G 12;
AH 9; 1 B 9; 2 B 6; for han see 'Impure Rime' below;
1 ps. pl. E 3204; G 2735.   Infin. lân E 47; I 52; G 2;
AH 3; 1 B 7; 2 B 2; (inf. lâzen E 3; I 2; AH 2; 1 B 2,
reading lâzen: erlâxen ll. 1027·8.)   past part. lân E
21; I 22; G 3; AH 2; 1 B 1; 2 B 1; (part. lâzen E 777,
9127; I 2025.)   other forms in ân: 1 ps. sg. E 9345; lâze,
1 ps. sg. ind. G 2410) 1 ps. pl. E 903; 3 ps. pl. subj. E 7636.
Inf. stân E 49; I 36; G 11; AH 5; 1 B 3; 2 B 3; 1 ps.
sg. E 5701; AH 1, 746; 2 B 135, 676; 3 ps. pl. subj. E 7637;
no past part. in ân; (part. -standen E 1432, 9497.   For
ên see below.   Inf. enpfân E 3560; I 1667, 4000, 7794;
AH 634; inf. vervân E 6228; G 465; also L 204,a;
vervân — past part. L 208,a.)   inf. slân I 4290; vo
pfâhen E 10011; 1 B 419; vâhen E 9777; I 1342,
1482, 8275; gevâhen I 2309; G 951; 2 B 4.   embe-
vâhen I 7508).

[4] Cf. zwâre p. 13.

[5] gât E 6; I 9; G 9; AH 3; 1 B 11; 2 B 3.   hât E
31; I 25; G 23; AH 1; 1 B 13; 2 B 9.   lât E 9; I 3; G 3.
AH 1; 1 B 7; 2 B 9.   stât E 26; I 19; G 12; AH 2; 1 B

G 59; AH 7; 1 B 35; 2 B 13. (hâte[1] E 10; G 5; AH 2;
hâten E 5; G 2; AH 1).

naeme[2] E 26; 1 1; G 7; AH 3; 1 B 3. nomen[2] E 7.
naere[3] E 76; I 83; G 66; AH 11; 1 B 16; 2 B 8. acte[4]

13; 2 B 5. hât:rât E 9; I 15; G 8; 1 B 8; 2 B 3.
vervât— 3 ps. sg. E 906; 2 B 572 (empfâhet G 156).
(Leich: gelât — geladet 1765; schât — schadet 1761; vervât - 3 ps. sg. 1769). The large number of rimes in ât in
Gregorius is due to missetât which occurs in rime 25
times.

[1] Other âte-rimes E 5; I 9; G 6; AH 1; 1 B 1. Other
âten-rimes E 9; I 8; G 3; AH 3. Abundant occasion,
therefore, in Iwein for the use of this preterit form in rime.
It will be noticed that this is not the case with the 1. or 2. B.
The references are: hâte E 154, 1499, 2546, 2687, 4320,
4724, 4892, 6744, 6853, 7438; G 2099, 2457, 2496, 3307,
3412; AH 1237, 1345. hâten E 367, 914, 3948, 5253,
7041; G 2253, 3198; AH 1401. As to hete(n), not found
in rime in Hartman, I cannot agree with either Henrici (on
Iwein 31) or Schröder (ZfdA. XXXVIII, 98), but this is a
question of Middle High German Grammar rather than of
Hartman-criticism. I hope soon to have occasion to discuss
this elsewhere. It may be pointed out however that hete,
which Schröder (p. 98) calls "eine junge, nach analogie von
tete-tâten aus dem plural hâten erschlossene analogie-
form" occurs 22 times (ind. and subj.) in rime in Gottfried
von Strassburg, a fact overlooked also by Weinhold, Mhd.
Gramm. §394. For haete see below.

[2] naeme(n) in rime (cpds. included) E 27; I 1; G 4;
1 B 3. quaeme(n) (and cpds.) E 27; G 4; 1 B 1.
naeme(n):quaeme(n) (with their cpds.) E 25; G 4;
1 B 1. zaeme (and cpds.) E 7; I 1; G 1; AH 1; 1 B 2.
-aemen forms all of (ver)naemen:(be)quaemen.
See note on -am. There are no rimes in oeme.

[3] The high percentage of Gregorius is due to such rime-
words as sündaere, vischaere, swaere.

[4] haete in rime E 13; I 2; G 7; 1 B 5. Plural form
only E 4524 (as above). taete (and cpds.) in rime E 15;
I 9; G 9; AH 3; 1 B 2. haete and taete also Leich
1854 and 1856.

E 27; I 12; G 17; AH 3; 1 B 7.   actou E 1; G 2.
(haetont:taetont E 4524).

  ebte E 5.   obten E 1.   oc¹¹ E 34; G 1.   (er-
schrecket—part. :erwecket—part. E 6596.) (mege¹¹
—Subj. of mac, I 1043, 7144, 7208, 7405; 2 B 323. (en
mogon—3 p. pl. Ind. E 5769.) (en megt—2 ps. pl. Ind.
E 4637.) (johon:geschen E 11; I 3; AH 2; 1 B 2.
johen:geschehen E 9; I 3; G 2; 1 B 2; 2 B 3.
gejohen:geschehen E 6; I 1; G 1.   sehen:ge-
schehen E 7; I 19; G 6; AH 4.   ersehen:ge-
schehen E 8; I 2; 1 B 1.)   (knoht^a:reht E 5; I 4;
G 4; 1 B 1; 2 B 1.)   (knohte³:rehte E 26; I 2; 1 B
2.)   (welle(n)⁴ E 11; I 3; G 1; 1 B 1.)   (gevellet-
part. E 934, 5934.)   (dem:nem I 5207.   dem:wem I
7757.   don:otewon I 4517.)   ende E 20; I 3; G 8;
AH 2.   (endet:geschendet(part.) E 9360.   endet:
bewendet (part.) E 10110.   verendet:verpfondet
(part.) I 7719.   gewendet:geschendet (part.) G
1528.)   or⁵ E 30; I 48; G 8; 1 B 2.   (orde:werde E 8;
I 3; G 4; AH 2; 2 B 2.)   ort E 16; I 26; G 5; AH 3;
1 B 6; 2 B 2.   (gort⁶ E 4; I 15; G 2; AH 1; 1 B 5; 2 B
2.)   (herze(n):suerze(n)⁷ E 3; G 3; AH 3; 1 B 1;

---

[1] Érec:wec E 31; Érec:enwec E 4; Érec:
burewec 2.

[2] Iwein 1043, 7144, 7208, 7405; 2 B 323.   For mahte
and mähte see mac under Diction.   Cf. muge below.

[3] Cf. knoht p. 23.

[4] The rime-words are helle, geselle, zellen, all
with umlaut-e.   So helt:welt I 2163, 2569; welt:
twelt E 3914, 9324; G 3923.

[5] hër:wör E 2; I 3.   her:wer E 1; I 15; G 3.

[6] ich gor is found E 20; I 31; G 15; AH 6; 1 B 6;
2 B 3.

[7] E 5330, 5430, 8334; G 209, 431, 809; AH 379, 475,
1091; 1 B 437; 2 B 677.

2 B 1.) esen[1] E 6; I 18; G 10; AH 8; 1 B 1. (esse: wesse—pret. of wizzen E 6786.) (weste[2] E 3; I 12; G 6; AH 1.) (westen[2] E 3; G 1; AH 1.) (gester: swester[3] E 1344: I 4738. gester:vester E 6468. swester:vester G 237, 299, 449, 837. swestern: vestern E 7772.) ete[1] E 9; I 36; G 10; AH 4; 2 B 2. (ergetzet—part. :ersetzet (—part. E 6249, 9777) E 6248, 7274, 9776. letzet:ontsetzet—part. G l. 17).

ê[5] E 28; I 40; G 35: AH 7; 1 B 15; 2 B 10; (Vrien: stên I 4183. gên:bestên E 1366. Vriênes:ich verstênes I 2111.) êre[6] E 64; I 68; G 24; AH 5; 1 B 23; 2 B 7. êren[7] E 5; I 15; G 5; AH 3; 1 B 1; 2 B 1. êrte[7] E 6; I 11; G 2: AH 2. (gêt:stêt 1 B 95; I 4035. ergêt:verstêt 1 B 1579.)

[1] genesen:wesen E 3; I 9; G 5; AH 4; 1 B 1. genesen:gewesen E 2; I 8; G 1; AH 1. Inf. wesen (ent-) in rime: E 5; I 10; G 6; AH 7; 1 B 1; for sîn see below.

[2] The rime-words are beste, geste, veste, besten, gesten, engesten, all with umlaut-e.

[3] Paul on Gregorius 67 (large edition) does not give the complete statistic. It is perhaps worth noticing that these words, gester and swester, rime with umlaut-e in Erec and Gregorius only.

[4] Lûnete:(ge)bete I 8. Lûnete:(ge)tete I 14. The other rime-pairs are, bete:tete E 5; I 9; G 4; AH 3; 2 B 2; bete:ontete E 2; bete:getete E 1; I 3; G 2; AH 1. gebete:tete I 1; G 3; gebete: getete G 1; mete:tete E 1; Henete:tete I 1.

[5] The high percentage of Gregorius is due to sê (23 times). For mê and mêre (including their cpds.) the statistics are: mê E 18; I 27; G 19; AH 3; 1 B 8; 2 B 7; mêre E 46; I 42; G 15; AH 4; 1 B 16; 2 B 4. Altogether mê is found, E 34; I 46; G 29; AH 9; 1 B 13; 2 B 8; mêre E 79; I 65; G 23; AH 5; 1 B 25; 2 B 9.

[6] For mêre see note on ê. êre:sêre E 12; I 20; G 2; AH 1; 1 B 4; 2 B 1.

[7] See kêren p. 22.

eide[1] E 27; I 15; G 11; AH 5; 2 B 4.   eiden[2] E 13; I 13; G 16; AH 4; 1 B 5; 2 B 3.   eis[3] E 22; I 7u; G 12; AH 1; 2 B 1.   eine E 14; I 4; G 1u; AH 2; 1 B 4; 2 B 1.   eise[4] E 5; G 5. (seist : weist 1 B 443. geseist : weist 1 B 1199. treist : weist I 3543; AH 1951 (enweist); 1 B 1413.) eit[5] E 147; I 169; G 55; AH 26; 1 B 20; 2 B 19. eite[6] E 16; I 5; G 5; AH 1; 1 B 1.

ich[7] E 40; I 69; G 6; AH 26; 1 B 13; 2 B 4.   ieh-

---

[1] See hoide.

[2] beiden and scheiden (and cpds.) cause the high percentage of Gregorius.

[3] Iwein in rime I 42 times. Gâwein E 5; I 15. For oeboin see 'Impure Rime.' For Gregorius bein and stein come in for consideration; so with eine.

[4] See froise p. 36.

[5] -heit (-keit) abstracts in rime: E 73; I 96; G 30; AH 13; 1 B 12; 2 B 14.   Contracted forms in ei in rime as follows: geleit — partic. (and cpds.) E 23; I 30; G 19; AH 4; 1 B 1 (also Leich 1651); 2 B 1; (geileite — pret. E 286 (?), 3055; I 954; G 191, 1810, 2327, 2480; seit (3 ps. sg.) (and cpds.) E 9; I 7; 1 B 2 (also Leich 1669); 2 B 1; geseit — partic. (and cpds.) E 18; I 34; G 12; AH 5; 1 B 2; 2 B 3; seite (pret.) E 3058, 3384, 3661, 4002, 7462, 7476; G 2479; (vor)treit (3 ps. sg.) E 1; I 8; G 3; 1 B 2 (also Leich 1667); 2 B 2.   For participles of verbs in eiden and eiten the statistics are: ungebeit E 1764; gebreit E 376; G 1055; zerbreit E 2309, 7718, 7751, 7861, 8727 (Bech besproit); gekleit (Lachmann's references, note on I 308, cited by Henrici, are not complete) E 13, 1951, 1982, 8228, 8938, 9878; geleit E 407 (h), 6485; gespreit E 368, 8600; G 710, 848, 999; gespreitet (: verleitet, 3 ps. sg.) AH 731.

[6] Inflected forms of -heit (-keit) abstracts in rime E 4; I 1; G 1. For seite see Note 5.

[7] Taking the editions as they stand. Pronominal forms, ich, mich, dich, sich, in rime, E 58; I 102; G 10; AH 25 (8 times with Heinrich); 1 B 23; 2 B 10. Statistics for some of the rime-couplets are : ich : mich E 7; I 29;

en[1] I 4; G 4; 2 B 1. (wider(e) E 6081 (hin-); I 7 *times*.)
igen E 5; I 11; G 6. iht E 36; I 43; G 12; AH 5; 1 B
17; 2 B 10. in[2] E 38; I 73; G 27; A H 17; 1 B 10; 2 B 6.
inne[2] E 24; I 37; G 8; AH 3; 1 B 11; 2 B 8. (kint:sint

AH 1; 1 B 2; 2 B 1. mich:sich E 2; I 9; G 1; AH 1;
2 B 2. For rich(—rîch): sich, E 1944 see 'Impure
Rime'. -lich forms in rime, with short vowel: E 18; I 30;
G 2; AH 15 (4 times with Heinrich, which nowhere rimes
with i); 1 B 3; 2 B 2. Of the thirty cases in Iwein, however,
ten should be written with i, though both Lachmann and Henrici write i. They are identical rimes of gelich with other
-lich adjectives: 427 (:cislich), 615 (mislich), 753
(tägelich), 1684 (: wünneclich), 2659 (unmügelich;
Bech here has i). Of the above companion-rimes two are elsewhere actually found joined to undoubted ich-words: mis-
lich:rich I 2579; tägelich:vroudenrîch G 1971.
What practically proves the length of i in these cases, is the
fact that it is nowhere in Iwein joined in rime with a pronominal
ich-form. *All* the remaining twenty cases of -lich in rime in
Iwein are so joined, the distribution being: ich 3 times; dich
2 times; mich 11 times; sich 4 times. In Erec, on the
other hand, there are three instances of gelich in rime: 299
(:sich), 2759 (:ich), 2873 (:sich). As gelich with long
or short vowel, occurs in rime no less than 32 times in Hartman,
(or including ungelich, 40 times) and is, outside of Erec,
nowhere found joined to a rime-word with undoubted short i,
it cannot be put on a level with other -lich adjective-forms.
Cf. Zarncke, Nibel. CXXXI, Note *), where, however, a
wrong conclusion is drawn. Identical rimes in -lich in Erec
and Zweites Büchlein have all been written with i by Haupt:
see ich-rimes below.

[1] Adverbs in -lichen in rime I 2480, 4200, 4296, 4724;
G 3471. Cf. ichen.

[2] in:hin E 3; I 27; G 4; AH 3. in:sin E 3; I 16;
G 6; AH 5; 1 B 1; 2 B 2. In rime altogether in (adv.) E 6;
I 7; G 7; AH 3; in (acc. sg. pron.) E 8; I 29; G 8; AH 5;
1 B 1; in (dat. pl.) E 8; I 23; G 6; AH 6; 1 B 1; 2 B 2;
hin E 9; I 34; G 6; AH 4. Total number of occurrences
of hin: E 50 (MS and Bech three additional passages); I 64;
G 17; AH 13; 1 B 1; 2 B 1. Proper nouns (see also 'Impure
Rime') that rime with i as well (see i and in): in: Imâin E

E 7; I 14; G 19; AH 6; 1 B 1; 2 B 1.) i⁰⁾ E 16; 1 28; G 10; AH 19; 1 B 14; 2 B 7. 1ₛₜ⁰⁾ E 16; 1 30; G 15; AH 19; 1 B 15; 2 B 7.

i¹⁾ E 33; 1 46; G 8; AH 3; 1 B 11; 2 B 10. i b⁓⁾ E 24; 1 7; G 9; AH 5; 1 B 9; 2 B 6. i ch⁓⁾ E 27; 1 11; G 7; AH 3; 2 B 2. i ch e⁶⁾ E 46; 1 4; G 10; AH 2; 1 B 3, 2 B 1. i ch e n⁷⁾ E 26; 1 10; G 2; AH 5; 1 B 4; 2 B 1. (m l l ⁜

176, 1316; Keiin:biu E 4694, 4780; Kelin:bin E 4890. Feminines in -in (-inne, in): in: meigerin AH 1487; in: kūnegin I 59, 77, 97; bin: kuneginn E 3364. The statement of Weinhold (Mhd. Gramm. § 274) is not entirely correct. -inne forms in rime: kuneginne E 5245; I 4587, 7506; AH 812; vriundinne E 1297, 6475, 9487; viondinne I 1423, 1542, 1665 (t.ä.t); dorftiginne E 694; I 6403; meisterinne E 5890; I 1626; gotinne E 5161; (also Leich 1844); süennerinne I 2056; fürstinne 2 B 284; verrätaerinne I 4046.

¹⁾ Pronominal forms (mir, dir, wir, ir) in rime E 27; I 46; G 17; AH 28; 1 B 28; 2 B 13. (irz: mirz I 6013).

²⁾ ist in rime E 15; I 29; G 14; AH 6; 1 B 13; 2 B 7. See also frist p. 36.

³⁾ Keii (see in and in) in rime I 9 times. ei (subj.) E 31; I 41; G 7; AH 8; 1 B 11; 2 B 10. ei (pron.) E 11; I 9; AH 1; 1 B 4.

⁴⁾ libe:wibe E 19; I 7; G 7; AH 2; 1 B 1; 2 B 5.

⁵⁾ -lich forms in rime: E 39 (22 of these identical rimes; all but one before l. 2500: 288, 744, 844, 1390, 1452, 1910, 2236, 2302, 2318, 2322, 9252; non-identical: 332, 2340, 3199, 3822, 3988, 5980, 6245, 6470, 9373, 9792); I 11 (3 identical: 1334, 1670, 8596, all with subst. lich; non-identical: 2670, 3169, 3358, 3590, 3575, 4208, 6269, 6624); G 7 (1 eb — subst.: gelich 2928; non-identical: 901, 1045, 1273, 1916, 1972, 2034); AH 8 (43, 199, 281; 2 B 4 (all identical: 77, 175. Cf. the note on rimes in ich.

⁶⁾ -liche forms in rime E 60 (28 of these identical rimes: 782, 2458, 2898, 2940, 2960, 3336, 4396, 4854, 5094, 5106, 5744, 7148, 7968, 9740); I 5 (2 identical: 2217); G 13 (6 identical: 203, 2933, 3331); AH 3; 1 B 3 (2 identical: 909; 2 B 2 (identical: 171).

⁷⁾ Adverbs in -lichen in rime E 26 (4 of these identical: 904, 1946); I 11 (2 identical: 3755); G 2; AH 5; 1 B 4.

wile E 7; I 2; 2 B 1.) in[1] E 121; I 32; G 18; AH 9;
1 B 20; 2 B 3. (lip: wip E 51; I 59; G 22; AH 9; 1 B
10; 2 B 5.) (gist: list 1 B 319; gîst: sîst E 5782,
5916; list: verpflîst 1 B 695; lîst: sîst 1 B 475.)
(git—gibot E 7; I 4; 1 B 1.) (lit—liget; including
ver-ge; E 9; I 7; G 4; 1 B 2.) (sit: zît E 14; I 6;
G 1.) ite[2] E 20; I 5. iten[2] E 67; I 15; G 5; 2 B 3.
iz[3] E 15; G 1. îze E 4; G 2; 2 B 1.

io[4] E 80; I 32; G 32; AH 4; 1 B 6; 2 B 2. (iemen:
riemen E 2410. niemen: (wâfen) riemen E
3076, 4414, 9390; I 319.) ienc[4] E 2; I 15; 2 B 1.

[1] Infinitive sin in rime E 92 (4 of these gesin); I
25; G 15; AH 9; 1 B 18; 2 B 3. Subj. and Ind. sin E 1;
I 1; 1 B 1. Pronominal forms (mîn, dîn, sin) E 24;
I 18; G 10; AH 6; 1 B 16; 2 B 2. 1 mâin (: vriundin
and sin) E 7. Keiin (: mîn and sin) E 5. Feminines
in -in (-in, -inne): künegin E 28 times (: vriundîn,
menigin, min, (ge)sin, schin, trehtin); I 5
(: mîn, sin); vriundîn E 9 times (: Imâin, künc-
gin, getwergelîn, sin, schin). Total number of
occurrences of künegin (inne, in) in Hartman: E 41;
I 20; AH 1.

[2] Frequency in Erec due to Ênîte.

[3] Cf. vlîz, wiz pp. 36 and 39.

[4] gie (including cpds.) E 58 (with preterit of vâhen
and its cpds. 16 times; with hie—hienc once); I 10 (: enpfie once); G 19 (with pret. of vâhen 6 times); AH 3
(: enpfie once); 1 B 1 (: enpfie); 2 B 2 (: gevie).
gienc (and cpds.) E (: vienc) 6688, 7316; I 14 times (including cpds.; all with preterit of vâhen and its cpds.
Henrici and L.[4] agree except for l. 3791 where L.[4] reads enpfie:
gie); 2 B 542 (: vervienc). vie, enpfie etc. E 26
(16 times with gie and cpds.; once with hie—hienc);
I 1 (: ergie); G 7 (6 times with gie and cpds.); AH 1
(: ergie); 1 B 1 (: ergie); 2 B 1 (: begie). vienc
etc. E 2 (: gienc); I 15 (14 times with gienc and cpds.;
once with gehienc); 2 B 541 (: begienc). hie (—hienc)
E 5410 (: knie), 7743 (: gie), 8952 (: vie); erhie G
2625 (: hie, adv.). gehienc I 4674 (: gevienc). lie

ieret[1] E 9; I 1.

och[2] I 6; G 1; AH 3; 1 B 1; 2 B 1. (mohte[3]:tohte E 6; I 6; G 8; AH 2.) (mohten E 3; I 2.) (enmohter:tohter E 1848; G 1081; AH 591.) olde[4] E 25; I 14; G 13. olden[4] E 2; I 3; AH 1. (von, dávon, dorvon E 1; I 6; G 5; 2 B 2) (vone:wone E 8886; G 561; 1 B 1547; 2 B 735.)

(mohte[5], enmohte:tohte, entohte E 3; I 7; G 3; AH 4; 2 B 1.)

ô[6] E 69; I 40; G 24; AH 13; 1 B 8; 2 B 8. ôst[7] E 4; I 2; G 2; AH 1; 1 B 3; 2 B 1. ôste[7] E 1; I 11. (nôt:tôt E 22; I 41; G 17; AH 21; 1 B 8; 2 B 7.) ôz E 30; I 15; G 17; AH 8; 2 B 1.

Ê 14; I 7; G 6; 1 B 1; 2 B 1. liez E 8; I 7; G 2; AH 2; 1 B 1. hie (adverb) in rime E 16; I 23; G 17; AH 1; 1 B 2.

[1] See zieren, parrieren, pungieren etc. under Diction.

[2] (ie)doch I 6; G 1; AH 2; 1 B 1; 2 B 1. (dan)noch I 6; G 1; AH 3; 2 B 1.

[3] See mac under Diction and cf. môhte.

[4] See golt p. 19. golde:solde E 7; I 3; G 6; :wolde E 1; solde:wolde E 16; I 10; G 7; ensolde:enwolde I 1. solden:wolden E 1; I 3; AH 1 (en-). soldest:woldest E 1. soldet:woldet I 1. erholte:solte I 2795; solte:wolte AH 439, 957; 1 B 1525 (enwolte); 2 B 531. engolten:solten 1 B 117. vergolten:solten I 5345.

[5] See mac under Diction and cf. mohte(n).

[6] dô in rime E 51; I 18; G 11; AH 10; 1 B 1; 2 B 1. dô:vrô E 31; I 9; G 7; AH 3; 2 B 1. hô as adj. (see Lachmann on Iwein 617) E 7341, 9015; G 734; as adv. E 1432, 7661, 10040; I 7081. hôch:vlôch I 3771.

[7] -lôst (past participle) (:trôst, untrôst) E 6095, 6563, 8821, 9605; I 6371, 6862; G 3776; AH 178; 1 B 260, 844, 1104; 2 B 665. lôste (pret.) (and cpds.) E 8142 (:untrôste pret.); I 4161, 4955, 5162, 6028, all with (misse)trôste— preterit; 4519, 4715, 5356, 5835, 6769, 7787, all with trôste—dative: 7872 (:rôste).

gehoenet -part. : gekroenet—part. 2 B 701.
gekroenet— part. : geschoenet— part. E 8270.) ge-
froeret— indic. : ungehoeret- part. 1 B 467. ge-
hoeret--part. : zerstoeret— part. E 7550.

(houbet[1] : geloubet E 8516, 8786, 9572; I 429,
4261; : beroubet E 868, 1580, 9392; : betoubet
E 770, 5734, 9122.) ouwen[2] E 26; I 10; G 4; 2 B 2.

(dreu:leu 1 6693. dreun:leun I 6109. ge-
dreun:leun I 5263, 6257, 6867. keun:leun I
6687. leun:gevreun[3] I 5501.)

(jugent:tugent E 2; I 10; G 3; AH 1; 2 B 4.)
(hulde:schulde E 1; I 12; G 5. hulden:schul-
den E 1: I 6: G 1; AH 3.) unde[4] E 33; I 16; G 18;
AH 8; 1 B 8: 2 B 4. unden[4] E 29; I 29; G 11; AH 5.
under[5] E 12; I 4; G 2; AH 1; 2 B 1. (zerunne[6]
subj.: sunne— subst. 2 B 17.) (kunt:stunt E 11; I 5;
G 2; AH 1: 1 B 2.) us[7] E 5; G 14: AH 1. (brust[8] —
dat:gelust E 8982; bruste—acc. pl. : luste—pret.
E 9310; brusten:kusten E 5756—kuste in, 9112.)

(lüge:müge[9] 2 B 511. müge:tüge I 7985.)
(sünde G 6. sünden G 3. sündet G 2.) (günne—
subj. : wünne—subst. E 9948. künne—subj. : wünne
I 3973. wünne:gewünne[10]—subj. E 5626.) (tür[11]:
vür I 9; G 1; AH 2.) (brüste — acc. pl. : küste—pret.

---

[1] Cf. Henrici on Iwein 430.
[2] All schouwen:vrouwen with their compounds.
[3] Overlooked by Henrici in note to Iwein 3840.
[4] See beginnen and stunde under Diction.
[5] See besunder p. 11.
[6] Cf. ünne below.
[7] See sus und alsus.
[8] Lachmann on Iwein 462. See brüste(n) below.
[9] Cf. mege above.
[10] Cf. unne above.
[11] tor:vor E 2: I 5; G 2; AH 1. :dervor I 1.
burgetor:vor E 6; I 6; G 3.

E 6792[1]. b r u s t e n : l u s t e n - inf. E 7354. b r ü s t e n :
g e l u s t e n - dat. pl. E 6112; : g e l u s t e n - inf. 1 B
63.)

(d û : n û G 2; AH 2; 1 B 2; 2 B 1. n û : b i s t û 1 2.)
(r û m d e : e n s û m d e 1 6983.) (g e b û r e : u n t û r e G
2791.) û s[2] E 11; 1 18. û s e[2] E 8; 1 1. (b û w e : g e -
t r û w e G 523. b û w e n : g e t r û w e n G 2689. g e r û w e :
g e t r û w e 1 B 87.)

i n w e[3] E 8; 1 4; G 4; AH 3; 1 B 1. i n w e n[3] E 10;
1 3; G 4; 1 B 1; 2 B 1.

(t u o, *with cpds.* E 10; 1 15; G 2; AH 5; 1 B 18; 2 B
3.) u o e E 44; 1 39; G 11; AH 2. u o n[4] E 4; 1 B 1.
(t u o s t, *with cpds.* E 2; 1 1; AH 2; 1 B 3.) (g u o t : m u o t
E 37; 1 44; G 25; AH 16; 1 B 9; 2 B 2. t u o t *with cpds.*
E 24; 1 24; G 4; AH 2; 1 B 19; 2 B 6.) (g u o t e :
m u o t e E 14; 1 11; G 16; AH 2; 1 B 2; 2 B 6.) (h u o -
t e r — h u o t e e r : m u o t e r E 10118.

(g u o t e : g e m ü e t e E 5; 1 12; G 2; AH 7; 1 B 1.)

---

[1] So Haupt. Compare, however, Lachmann on Iwein
462. See b r u s t above.

[2] h û s — dat. E 8; 1 15; h û s e — dat. E 8; 1 1. The
accompanying rime-words are A r t û s, A r t û s e, and (once)
m û s.

[3] See also û w e above. The statistic of Bock (Q. u. F.
XXXIII, 54) for the rimes r i u w e (n) : t r i u w e (n) in Hartman calls for correction. He omits E 3668, 4084 (cf. 4286,
which he cites). For Gregorius he has taken no account of
the Spiezer MS (PBB III), in which the introduction is pre-
served, and has hence omitted ll. 75, 125. For Der arme
Heinrich he has overlooked ll. 819, 1001. In the case of the
Erstes Büchlein ll. 37, 55 should be added. 2 B 277 he has
also not noted.

[4] Four rime-pairs with r u o n; the other is h u o n : g e -
t u o n E 2042.

IDENTICAL RIME.

The subject of identical[1] rime ('rührender reim') in Hartman has, to my knowledge, been treated in three places: by Wilhelm Grimm in Zur Geschichte des Reims (Abh. der Berl. Akad. 1851, pp. 521-713; also separately Göttingen 1852), by Lemcke, Hartmann von Aue (Stettin Prog. 1862), and by Greve, Leben und Werke Hartmann's von Aue (Fellin Prog. 1879). None of these are satisfactory; they all omit a large part of the actual number of occurrences.

Identical rime may be defined as rime in which the riming syllables are identical in form. To a modern ear this kind of rime seems objectionable and we find that for the Middle High German poet too it did not occupy the same position as ordinary rime. This is clearly shown not only by its low ratio of frequency but also by the limitations with which its use was attended. Identical rime then may be regarded as by nature a makeshift, used mostly where there was a paucity or entire lack of other rimes. From this principle there follows that as the technical skill of the poet developed, his recourse to this makeshift would become less and less frequent. Alongside of this increase in the poets resources we must suppose that there was developing a finer feeling for the imperfections of this kind of rime: refinement of feeling for form went side by side with a greater versatility in the employment of resources at command. It must therefore be regarded as an especially valuable criterion in that it not only indicates development, but of itself points out the direction which this development must take. Simplicity of application, leaving little room for difference of opinion as to actual facts, is another of the advantages of this test. It is not to be denied that an artistic use of identical rime is possible; it may be so employed, but there are few traces of this in Hartman's works.

---

[1] For the present purpose it is not necessary to distinguish between 'identischer' and 'rührender' rime. The several categories are separated below.

Excluding, as heretofore, the songs, the statistic[1] for identical rime is as follows: Erec 110 rime-couplets; I 27: G 21; AH 3; 1 B 25 (including l. 1027); 2 B 5. For a correct valuation of these figures some changes will have to be made in the case of Iwein and the Erstes Büchlein, but from a formal point of view the table may stand for the present. Before classifying these rimes I give the references seriatim.

E 176, 202, 288, 468, 508, 738, 744, 782, 844, 904, 948, 1060, 1144, 1290, 1316, 1320, 1630, 1650, 1654, 1656, 1688, 1698, 1852, 1910, 1914, 1984, 1946, 1978, 2180, 2286, 2802, 2318, 2392, 2334, 2382, 2390, 2408, 2458, 2514, 2576, 2626, 2802, 2814, 2852, 2882, 2808, 2940, 2960, 3046, 3092, 3114, 3140, 3276, 3336, 3390, 3450, 3778, 3826, 4396, 4438, 4462, 4590, 4858, 4950, 5018, 5036, 5064, 5094, 5106, 5302, 5318, 5626, 5648, 5744, 5892, 6462, 6472, 6598, 6670, 6756, 6760, 6828, 7028, 7062, 7068, 7070, 7148, 7182, 7366, 7508, 7558, 7606, 7670, 7696, 7702, 7966, 7968, 8202, 8322, 8596, 8598, 8726, 8818, 9252, 9280, 9482, 9648, 9740, 9974, 10074.

I 87, 427, 615, 753, 1333, 1587, 1669, 1683, 1685, 2171, 2217, 2659, 3019, 3217, 3595, 3755, 4407, 5423, 6535, 6601, 6657, 7151, 7153, 7155, 7157, 7159, 7437.

G 203, 869, 931, 949, 1019, 1575, 1999, 2221, 2383, 2625, 2657, 2927, 2938, 2980, 2995, 3041, 3043, 3201, 3381, 3757, 3861.

AH 21, 689, 1099, 1199, 1243, 1267, 1357, 1453.

1 B 13, 168, 435, 525, 651, 815, 909, 917, 975, 1027 (MS and Bech), 1153, 1171, 1279, 1353, 1451, 1635;

---

[1] Grimm cites as follows: E 72; I 14; G 12; AH 4; 1 B 10; 2 B 5. Lemcke gives: E 72; I 12; G 11; AH 3; 1 B 9; 2 B 4. Greve: E 93; I 13; G 11; AH 6; 1 B 17; 2 B 5. That Lemcke is dependent on Grimm seems proved by his copying Grimm's misprint E 395 (= 4397). Greve has also used Lemcke to some extent as is shown by his citing E 5743 twice.

Leich[1]: 1651, 1713, 1714, 1730, 1749, 1864, 1865, 1872, 1880.
2 B 35, 77, 171, 175, 771.

The so-called 'Leich' should be separated from the rest of the Erstes Büchlein.   Alternate rimes running through systems of from four to thirty-two lines are essentially different from the ordinary rime-couplet and the change can at once be felt at l. 1645, the beginning of the 'Leich.'   The latter, counting only those adjacent, has 9 identical rimes, an average[2] of one to every 29 lines ; the 'Büchlein' proper has 16, an average of one to every 103 lines.   To class the two under one category would, therefore, only obscure the actual state of affairs.   Again, the five rime-couplets, Iwein 7151–60 (gulte:engulte; gelten:engelten; engiltet: giltet; engolten:vergolten; galt:engalt), so-called grammatical rimes, while formally identical, are conscious playing with language, and do not, therefore, belong to the category of identical rime proper.   Grimm, Lemcke and Greve have accordingly passed them over in silence under this head.   On the other hand, AII 167, mislich: genislich, even though a rime in lich, cannot be considered identical, as Grimm, Lemcke and Greve have done, since the accented character of the syllables mis and nis destroys the identity of the lich-endings.

Revising the table and computing the averages per 10.000 lines we have:

Erec[3] 110 - 108.8

---

[1] Line 1681, gewant with MS and Bech; so lande l. 1764.

[2] The 'Leich' contains 264 lines, not counting those lost.

[3] Deducting from the total number of lines the incomplete couplets (15, including the first), leaving 10106 lines. Some of these rime-pairs were no doubt identical, this fact explaining in part the cause of their omission: the eye caught the second rime-word just after the first had been written down.   This also explains why so many constitute the *second* line of the couplet, twelve out of the fourteen in the middle of the poem.

Iwein 22 — 26.9
Gregorius 21 — 52.4
Armer Heinrich[1] 8 - 51.9
Erstes Büchlein 16 — 97.3
Zweites Büchlein 5 — 60.5

These figures naturally carry most weight for the longer pieces, Erec, Iwein and Gregorius. That they are not without value, however, for the other poems, may be seen by comparing the average of each 500 lines in the several works:

	E	I	G	AH	1B	2B
1-500	4	2	1	1	3	4
500-1000	7	2	3	1	6	
-1500	5	1	1	6	6	
-2000	12	4	2			
-2500	10	2	2			
3000	10	1	6			
-3500	8	2	4			
-4000	2	2	2			
-4500	3	1				
-5000	3	0				
-5500	7	1				
-6000	4	0				
-6500	2	0				
-7000	5	3				
-7500	7	1				
-8000	8	0				
-8500	1					
-9000	5					
-9500	3					
-10000	3					

It will be seen that both Erec and Iwein show a decrease in the ratio of frequency in the second half: Erec from 64 to 45, Iwein from 16 to 6. Gregorius on the other hand shows an increase: from 7 to 14.

---

[1] Adding the lines marked *a*, *b*, *c*, *d*, in Paul's second edition, making 1540 lines in all.

In classifying, the following categories may be dis-
tinguished:

I. Foreign and proper nouns, constituting either one or
both parts of the rime-pair: E 176, 738, 1316, 1630, 1650,
1654, 1656, 1688, 1914, 1934, 2576, 2852, 2882, 3390,
4438, 5036, 7558, 8202; I 87; G 931, 1575, 1999, 3201;
AH 1199, 1357; 1 B 1279.

II. Forms in l i c h or l i c h: E 288, 744, 844, 1320,
1852, 1910, 2286, 2302, 2318, 2322, 9252; I 427, 615,
753, 1333, 1669, 1683, 2659, 3595; G 2927; 2 B 77, 175.

III. Forms in l i c h e: E 782, 2458, 2898; 2940,
2960, 3336, 4396, 4858, 5094, 5106, 5744, 7148, 7968,
9740; I 2217; G 203, 2933, 3331; 1 B 909; 2 B 171.

IV. Forms in l i c h e n: E 904, 1946, 2382, 2814,
3140; 1 3755; 1 B 651.

V. l i c h e z: E 7068.

VI. s c h a f t, s c h e f t e: E 1978, 2334, 7366, 7606.

VII. Complete identity of form, difference in syntactic
use or in meaning[1]: E 2390 (s i n — inf. : s i n — pron.), 2514
(i n — adv.: u m b i n — pron.), 2626 (d i c k e — adv.: d i c k e —
subst.), 3450 (l e i t — pret. : l e i t — subst.), 5892 (a r m e —
adj. : a r m e — subst.), 7062 (w â g e — peril : w â g e — billow),
7182 (w i l t — d û w i l t : w i l t — game), 9648 (i n — adv. :
i n - pron.); I 1587 (w i r t — subst. : w i r t — vb.); G 2383
(i n - adv. : i n - pron.), 3041 (idem), 3757 (l i u t e n — vb. :
l i u t e n — subst.); 1 B 1353 (d i n g e n — subst. : d i n g e n —
vb.), Leich 1730 (s w a e r e — subst. : s w a e r e — adj.), 1872
(r i n g e - adv. : r i n g e — vb.).

VIII. Identity: I 7437 (i c h : i c h); G 949[2] (g r ô z :
g r ô z); AH 1099 (z u o : z u o); 1 B 1451 (i c h : i c h); 2 B
771 (m i t e : m i t e).

---

[1] Compare also IX.

[2] See, however, Paul's note on l. 777 in his larger
edition.

IX. One rime-word identical with part of the other.

a) Simplex and compound: E 3276 (entwosen:wosen), 4590, (junkherren:herren), 5018 (vernam: nam), 5302 (idem), 8522 (eteswâ:wâ); I 2171 (vernement:nement), 3019 (bax:vurbaz), 3217(etewâ: wâ); 1 B 435 (nemen:vernemen), 525 (versolt: solt), 975 (unversolt:solt), 1027 (lâzen:erlâzen), 1171 (sô:alsô), 1635 (verneme:neme).

b) Others: E 202 (waere:sparwaere), 468 (id.), 508 (id.), 1060 (mite — *adv.*:vermite), 1290 (gunnen: begunnen), 2180 (wert — *subst.*:gewert), 2408 (gewant — *part.*:isengewant), 2802 (misselanc:lanc), 3046 (dinge:gedinge), 3092 (beroit:reit — *pret.*), 3114 (walt:gewalt), 3778 (gewert:wert — *adj.*), 4462 (lanc:gelanc), 4950 (wert — *adj.*:entwert), 5318 (leit — *subst.*:erleit — *vb.*), 5626 (wunne — *subst.*:gewunne), 5648 (vâlande:lande), 6472 (wert — *adj.*: gwert), 6598 (bâren:gebâren), 6670 (wunden — *subst.*:gewunden), 6756 (gwalt:walt), 6760 (walt: gewalt), 6828 (gewalt:walt), 7028 (gewar — *adj.*: war — *pret.*), 7070 (sant — *subst.*:gesant), 7702 (wol — *adv.*:boumwol), 7966 (lanc:gelanc), 8598 (rich: esterich), 8726 (breit:zerbreit), 9482 (heim: ocheim), 9974 (füere:gefüere — *adj.*), 10074 (gunnen:begunnen); I 1685 (leit — *subst.*:geleit — geleget), 5423 (überwunden:wunden — *subst.*), 6657 (bewart *part.*:wart); G 869 (wert — *adj.*:entwert), 1019 (waere:gewaere — *adj.*), 2221 (rât:hirât), 2625 (erhie:hie — *adv.*), 2657 (belibe:libe), 2995 (gedanc:danc), 3861 (waere:gewaere — *adj.*); AH 21 (belibe:libe), 1243 (gedanc:danc), 1267 (want: gewant — *part.*), 1458 (hirât:rât); 1 B 13 (begunde: gunde), 163 (maere — *subst.*:unmaere), 815 (verlôs: lôs), 917 (gedanc:danc); Leich 1651 (geleit — geleget:leit *adj.*), 1713 (sane — *subst.*:versane),

1714 (bewaere:waere), 1749 (enban:ban -- *subst.*),
1864 (gedinge:dinge *subst.*): 2 B 35 (mache:un-
gemache).

X. Parts preceding rime-syllables dissimilar.

a) Dissimilar prefixes: E 1144 (ennemest:verne-
mest), 3826 (genam:vernam), 7696 (geschen:er-
sehen), 8818 (genam:vernam); AH 689 (verlust:
gelust); Leich 1880 (belangen:gelangen).

b) Others: E 948 (verlôs:sigelôs), 1698 (künegin : menigin), 5064 (unhovebaere:enbaere),
6462 (handelunge:gelunge), 7508 (scharlachen:
erlachen), 7670 (stegereife : goltreife), 8596
(behangen -- *part.* umbehangen - *subst.*), 9280 (zer-
füere:gefüere - *subst.*); I 4407 (herzeleit:geleit -
geleget), 6535 (behüeten:vuhshüeten), 6601 (über-
want - *pret.* : gowant -- *part.*); G 2989 (îsenhalten:
behalten), 3043 (gehalten:îsenhalten); 1 B 1153
(misselunge:wandelunge), Leich 1865 (getân:
undertân).

IMPURE RIME.

The subject may be considered under four heads: 1. a:â.
2. i:î. 3. m:n. 4. Other consonantal inaccuracies.

1. For the views of Lachmann and Haupt on a:â rimes,
see their notes on Iwein 2112, 5521 and Erec 241. Lachmann's theory that all passages showing such rimes are corrupt,
lacks support. Whether these and other similar rimes in
Hartman, are to be accounted for on the score of dialect or of
inaccuracy in rime, may perhaps make a difference in editing,
but it can scarcely affect our present view of the matter. There
seems to be sufficient evidence for both dialectic shortening of
long vowels and for long and short vowel rimes. Compare
Henrici on Iwein 2668.

Erec 240 a n : h â n — 1 ps. sg.; 1604 k a n : h â n — 1 ps. sg.: 3304[1] m a n : h â n — 1 ps. sg.

Iwein[2] 2667[2] g a s t e s : h â s t e s; 5521 m a n : h â n — 1 ps. sg.

Gregorius 805 g a r : a l w â r (see Paul's note on l. 633 in his larger edition).

Erstes Buchlein 445 h â n — 1 ps. sg. : a n; 511 m a n : h â n (Haupt adopts the emendation of Lachmann, note on Iwein 5522); Leich 1741 h â n — 1 ps. sg. : e n k a n.

Lieder 212,[3] u n d e r t â n : g e w a n.

2. Erec 1944[4] r i c h : s i c h; 8940[5] h â r m i n : i n. Whether in view of these indubitable examples of i : i rimes, i is also to be retained in Î m â i n E 176, 1316 and in K e i i n E 4694, 4781, 4890, does not seem at all clear. To judge from the form K o i i, found 9 times in rime in Iwein, it would appear that we have a freedom of word-form rather than of rime in the case of these foreign names. Possibly the three rimes of g e l i c h with forms in short i in Erec (299, 2759, 2873) are also to be classed under the present head. Compare Note 7 on p. 53.

Erstes Buchlein 1265 b i n : s i n — *inf.* (Haupt adopts Lachmann's emendation; Bech also changes).

---

[1] It is worth noticing that l. 3305 is mere padding for the sake of rime. This may frequently be observed in the case of inaccurate rimes. Haupt's â in this line is no doubt a misprint; compare ll. 240 and 1604.

[2] Paul's proposals, to read m i n : G â w e i n l. 7567 and k ü n e g i n : I w e i n l. 8121, would introduce rimes unparalleled in Hartman.

[3] Lachmann emended into h i e : i e rimes: cf. Henrici ad loc. and Paul, PBB I, 372.

[4] Haupt has r i c h.

[5] One will search in vain through Hartman for such a combination as is offered in Lachmann's conjecture : e i n e n m a n t e l h â r m i n l a n g e n.

3. Erec[1] 434 stein:ochein; 900 tuon:ruon; 1406 ochein:Tulmoin; 1830 nam : man (Haupt changes); 4358 ruon:tuon; 5482 ruon:huon; 8018 ochein:schein; 9408 dehein:ochein; 9720 Tulmoin:ochein.

Gregorius 137 ahselboin:hein; 737 ochein: mein; 2977 hein:stein.

Erstes Büchlein 971 ruon:tuon.

These m : n rimes, while clearly dialectic, find a further explanation in the lack of rime-facilities for the endings in question. Thus in uom there is only ruom:heiltuom G 3767; in eim only heim:ocheim E 9482, identical it will be noticed. For Iwein, rimes with Îwein and Gâwein would have been convenient. It should be added, however, that the statistic for heim and ocheim, the two words concerned, is as follows: heim E 12 (*1); I 2; G 3 (*2); AH 6; I B 2. ocheim E *6; G *1.

4. Erec 1780 enlaste—*pret.* of leschen:glaste.

Iwein 3473 bestreich:sweic; 4431 phlac:eranch. Compare Paul, PBB I, 375, 382.

Henrici's note on Iwein 2668 may be compared for this entire subject. Some supplementary statements will be found under the heads mac and setze, pp. 24 and 30. An examination of the distribution of the forms there noted will tend to show that his statement "auch die verwendung solcher dialektreime für die chronologie der gedichte Hartmanns wird dadurch hinfällig" is too sweeping.

CONCLUSION.

The point of greatest interest at present in any discussion of the chronology of Hartman's works is the position of Gregorius. In recent years the tendency has been to place it after

---

[1] The statement of Naumann, ZfdA XXII,35, stands in need of correction.

Iwein. The newly discovered introduction of the Gregorius[1] has been cited as evidence for this view. It is, however, difficult to conceive how the clause "daz rieten mir minin (Zwierzina *im driu*) tumben jâr" could group under one head two works so far apart stylistically as Erec and Iwein.

Surveying the results so far gained, the following points of connection between Erec and Gregorius[2] may be observed. Under Diction: d r â t e, s c h i e r e, b e g á n, b e g i n n e, b e s u n d e r, b i d e r b e, b l a n c, b o e s e, b u r g a e r e, z w á r e, e i n e, e l l e n t h a f t, (d a z) e l l e n d e, e n d e, e n t s t â n, e r h e b e, e r s e t z e, e r t r i c h e, (i c h) i l e, g á n z l i c h e n, b e g a r w e, g e l i e p, g e l p f, g e n a e d e c l i c h e (n), g e n a e m e, g e t á n, g e s l á h t e, g e v e l l i c, g e f u o g e, w â t, t o n e (z i m, g e z i m), h e r z e n l i c h e (n), h e r z e r i u w e, h i n f e l, h o e r e : v e r n i m, i e g l i c h, i t e w i z, k ü n d e, k ü n n e, r u o m, l o b e b a e r e, m i c h l ü s t e t, m a c, m i n n e c l i c h e n, m i s s e w e n d e, m u o t v e s t e, n i e t e m i c h, r i n g e, r i t t e r l i c h e n, r i u w e c l i c h e n, s n e l e k e i t, s a m, s c h e n k e l f l i e g e n, s c h ô n e, b e s c h o u w e, s e t z e (g o s a t), s i d i n, s l e h t, s m e r z e, s t u n d e (sg.), s u r z e n g e l, u n b e w a r t, u r l i u g e, v l î z, -f r e i s e, w a l t e, â n e w â n, w a n n e n, w i s e l ô s, w o r t z e i c h e n, m i c h n i m t w ü n d e r, w u n s c h, z e h a n t (etc.) : z e s t u n t (etc.), i c h z e l, z a l, z i l.

The only evidence of any importance that runs counter to this is that of h a r t e as adverbial modifier of adjs. and advbs. Arranging the different works according to its frequency, the order would be: Erec, Erstes Büchlein, Zweites Büchlein, Iwein, Armer Heinrich, Gregorius, in which the proportion in AH and G is nearly the same, and twice that of Iwein.

---

[1] Schönbach, p. 455.

[2] It seemed needless to repeat here the statistics already given under the separate heads of the first part. They are given in the order in which they occurred there.

Or arranging according to the ratio between h a r t e and v i l: Erec, Erstes Buchlein, Iwein, Armer Heinrich, Zweites Büchlein, Gregorius, in which the figures for I and AH are approximately equal, while G, leaving the 2 B out of consideration on account of the smallness of the numbers involved, shows an abnormally high percentage. Perhaps a study of other particles used to strengthen adjectives will somewhat modify this picture; it certainly seems a subject deserving attention.

As observed before, the results of the examination of rime-vowels are largely negative. The Büchlein first of all stand quite apart and should not be considered in one category with the epics: the percentage of *i*-rimes in the Erstes Büchlein as compared with Erec would alone determine that. Nor can any great importance be attached to rime-vowels whose percentage to the whole does not anywhere exceed that of five. This would exclude i e, ö, o e, o u, ö u, u, ü, û, i u, ü e. Of the eleven remaining vowels, â, ê, e i, o, u o do not show enough variation to serve as a basis for an argument, not even one of a cumulative character, when we consider the number of different factors that go to make up the average of a single vowel. Three others show a somewhat high ratio of frequency in only one work: a e in Gregorius, e and ô in Der arme Heinrich. These deviations are adequately explained, however, for Gregorius by the characteristic words, s ü n d a e r e, v i s c h a e r e, R ô m a e r e, s w a e r e, r i h t a e r e; for Der arme Heinrich, in the case of e, by S a l e r n e, g e n e s e n, l e b e n; in the case of ô, by t ô t (23 times). For the remaining vowels the statistics are: a E 27.466; G 25.861; I 25.227; AH 17.124; i E 7.459; G 9.186; I 11.952; AH 13.595; i E 10.852; I 6.27; AH 5.621; G 5.092. In these figures the small variation between Gregorius and Iwein for *a* is of no consequence, while the low percentage of Der arme Heinrich, on the other hand, is remarkable. So also for *i*, although there the words H e i n r i c h (12 times) and k i n t (9 times) might be considered special, which would bring the average below that of Iwein. For i the particulars are entered under rime-groups: no importance is to be attached to the slight variations between Iwein, Der arme Heinrich and Gregorius. Of some value[1], therefore, these results may be, in the case of *a* for the position of Der arme Heinrich, in the case of *i* for that of Gregorius.

Proceeding to a consideration of rime-groups, the statistic of the following endings and rime-couplets seem of importance for the position of Gregorius: a m (n a m, q u a m), a n d e (s a n d e, w a n d e, at, q u a m e n, h a t e, h a t e n, q u a o- m e (n), h a e t e, g e s t e r, s w e s t e r, s e i t e, g e b r e i t, g e s p r e i t, pronominal forms in -i c h[2], i n, i n: h i n, i c h e, s i n[4] (inf.), g i e[4]: g i e n e, r i e[4]: v i e n e, l i e: l i e z.

It seems unnecessary to recapitulate here the results reached under the head of Identical Rime. Attention may be called, however, to the position of Gregorius under the categories represented most numerously in Erec: IX*b*, I, III, II,

---

[1] Compare Kochendörffer's statistics (ZfdA XXXV, 291) of feminine rimes in Hartman, which do not furnish any possible basis for grouping.

[2] The difference is not due to the absolute frequency of the forms in question: i c h, m i c h, d i c h, s i c h. They are approximately as common in Gregorius as in Iwein; I have counted 1526 cases in Iwein and 569 in Gregorius. The case is different with rimes in i r. There the pronominal forms are absolutely more frequent in Iwein than in Gregorius, the proportion of instances in rime being as follows: E 1 : 34.6; I 1 : 19; G 1 : 16.5; AH 1 : 8.2; 1 B 1 : 11.9; 2 B 1 : 9.2. For the Büchlein these figures have, of course, no special significance, in as much as the ratio of m i r- and d i r-rimes is altogether abnormal.

[3] To the statistic on p. 56, note 1, the total number of occurrences of the inf. s i n in Hartman might have been added: E 103 (*92); I 46 (*25); G 21 (*15); AH 13 (*9); 1 B 21 (*18); 2 B 10 (*3).

[4] Assuming that MSS and editions are to be trusted in this respect.

VII, X*b*. In all of these, with the exception of II, Gregorius stands closer to Erec than does Iwein.

Under the head of Impure Rime the m: n rimes alone deserve mention.

Many of the phenomena cited would doubtless individually carry little weight as criteria of chronology. In such matters it is often difficult to draw the exact line of demarcation between the characteristic and accidental. As before remarked evidence of this nature necessarily assumes a cumulative character.

The argument, it would seem, is considerably strengthened by the fact that the Erstes Büchlein shows in many particulars such a close agreement with Erec, notwithstanding the vast differences in subject between the two poems. Among the most striking of these are, under Diction: snelle, balt, behage:gevalle, mich belanget, bereite, blanc, deiswâr, doch, (daz) ellende, begarwe, gelpf, gemeit, genaedeclich, -zim:touc, harte, -hoere: vernim, ruom, manlichen, quele, saelekeit, saeldenlôs, -sam, schîn, schône, sene, gesat, tugenthaft, vâlant, valsch, versol, vergebene, freise, walte, âne wân, wandel, wîselôs, ich zel, zal, zesamene, zil.

Under Rime-groups: sande, quaemen, haete, wesen:sin, inf. sîn in rime.

Under Identical Rime, a percentage second only to Erec.

Under Impure Rime, agreement with Erec under every head. i : î rimes in Erec and Erstes Büchlein only.

Some difficulty is encountered in assigning a definite place to Der arme Heinrich. Its ratio of identical rimes is rather high: nearly equal to that of Gregorius; the number of six such rimes from ll. 1000–1500 is not equaled anywhere in Iwein; and the category (IX*b*) under which one-half of the total number falls is the very one represented best in Erec. On the other hand there are no impure rimes. Under rime-vowels, as pointed out above, the only noteworthy fact is the

abnormally low percentage of *a*-vowels. However, as there
is no marked tendency towards a gradual decrease in the number of *a*-rimes, no great importance can be attached to this fact.
Under rime-groups Der arme Heinrich agrees with Iwein in
the following particulars: q u a m, s a n d e, q u â m e n,
q u a e m e (n), l i e : l i e z. The following would seem to
favor a position before Iwein: h â t e (n), h i n, i c h e, i c h e n,
inf. s i n in rime, g i e : g i e n e, d ô. d â, -i c h and -i r
pronominal forms, might perhaps be used as arguments for a
position after Iwein. In diction agreement with Iwein, more
or less in contrast with presumably earlier works, is shown under the heads b e g a r w e, g e n i s t, k l e i t, h a r t e,
h o e r e : v e r n i m, m a h t e, f u r n a m e s, s c h ô n e, g e-
s a t, i c h z e l, z a l, z i l. Usage in regard to the following
words favors a position before Iwein: b e g i n n e, z w â r e,
g e m e i t, g e n æ m e, h e r z e r i u w e, h e r z e s ê r e,
k u n n e, m i s s e w e n d e, -s a m, s m e r z e, s t u n d e,
t u g e n t l i c h e n, ü p p i c, w e r d e k e i t, m i c h n i m t
w u n d e r, z e h a n t : z e s t u n t, z o b e l. The evidence
accordingly seems to point strongly towards the order, Gregorius, Armer Heinrich, Iwein. I hope shortly to be able to
bring forward investigations of a stylistic character that will
strengthen this view, studies that it seemed less proper to introduce here because they can in no way lay claim to exhaustiveness, so far as the number of categories treated is concerned.

The Zweites Büchlein will be found to show no deviations
that would justify the supposition of spuriousness. In diction
it will usually be found agreeing either with the Erstes Buchlein or with Iwein, the former the result of similarity of theme,
the latter indicating in a general way the place that it occupies
chronologically: the pairs Erec, Erstes Büchlein and Iwein,
Zweites Büchlein may frequently be found thus grouped. The
poem is too short to warrant definite conclusions under the
several heads of rime technic.

Biographical Sketch.

I was born October 27, 1867, at Katwijk aan Zee, the Netherlands. After coming to America in the summer of 1881, I completed a course in the High School at Grand Rapids, Michigan, was matriculated at the University of Michigan in the autumn of 1885, and obtained the bachelor's degree in June, 1888. I then came to the Johns Hopkins University to pursue advanced courses in German, Greek and English. In January, 1889, I was appointed University scholar and from 1889–1891 held a fellowship in the department of German. In June, 1891, I went abroad to study at the University of Leipzig, remaining until February, 1892, when I returned to my work in Baltimore.

To my instructors both here and abroad, Professors Wood, Gildersleeve, Bright and Learned of the Johns Hopkins University, and Professors *Zarncke, von Bahder and Mogk of the University of Leipzig I wish to express my thanks, for manifold aid and encouragement. To Professor Gildersleeve I owe the first awakening of an interest in the closer study of syntax and style. To Professor Wood I owe a special debt: his personal interest and sympathy have never been wanting, while his broad scholarship and keen insight have served as a constant stimulus.

*Deceased.